# THE COMPLETE PARTNERSHIP BOOK

Edward A. Haman

Attorney at Law

**SPHINX® PUBLISHING**
AN IMPRINT OF SOURCEBOOKS, INC.®
NAPERVILLE, ILLINOIS
www.SphinxLegal.com

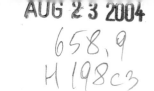
Third Edition, 2004

Published by: **Sphinx® Publishing, An Imprint of Sourcebooks, Inc.®**

Naperville Office
P.O. Box 4410
Naperville, Illinois 60567-4410
630-961-3900
Fax: 630-961-2168
www.sourcebooks.com
www.SphinxLegal.com

**Library of Congress Cataloging-in-Publication Data**
Haman, Edward A.
  The complete partnership book / by Edward A. Haman.
       p. cm.
  Includes index.
  ISBN 1-57248-391-1 (alk. paper)
  1. Partnership--United States--Popular works. 2. Partnership--United States--Forms. I. Title.

KF1375.Z9 H358 2004
346.73'0682--dc22
                              2004024877

Printed and bound in the United States of America.

VHG Paperback — 10 9 8 7 6 5 4 3 2 1

# Contents

# USING SELF-HELP
# LAW BOOKS

Before using a self-help law book, you should realize the advantages and disadvantages of doing your own legal work and understand the challenges and diligence that this requires.

**The Growing Trend**

Rest assured that you won't be the first or only person handling your own legal matter. For example, in some states, more than seventy-five percent of divorces and other cases have at least one party representing him or herself. Because of the high cost of legal services, this is a major trend and many courts are struggling to make it easier for people to represent themselves. However, some courts are not happy with people who do not use attorneys and refuse to help them in any way. For some, the attitude is, "Go to the law library and figure it out for yourself."

We at Sphinx write and publish self-help law books to give people an alternative to the often complicated and confusing legal books found in most law libraries. We have made the explanations of the law as simple and easy to understand as possible. Of course, unlike an attorney advising an individual client, we cannot cover every conceivable possibility.

**Cost/Value Analysis**

Whenever you shop for a product or service, you are faced with various levels of quality and price. In deciding what product or service to buy, you make a cost/value analysis on the basis of your willingness to pay and the quality you desire.

When buying a car, you decide whether you want transportation, comfort, status, or sex appeal. Accordingly, you decide among such choices as a Neon, a Lincoln, a Rolls Royce, or a Porsche. Before making a decision, you usually weigh the merits of each option against the cost.

When you get a headache, you can take a pain reliever (such as aspirin) or visit a medical specialist for a neurological examination. Given this choice, most people, of course, take a pain reliever, since it costs only pennies; whereas a medical examination costs hundreds of dollars and takes a lot of time. This is usually a logical choice because it is rare to need anything more than a pain reliever for a headache. But in some cases, a headache may indicate a brain tumor and failing to see a specialist right away can result in complications. Should everyone with a headache go to a specialist? Of course not, but people treating their own illnesses must realize that they are betting on the basis of their cost/value analysis of the situation. They are taking the most logical option.

The same cost/value analysis must be made when deciding to do one's own legal work. Many legal situations are very straight forward, requiring a simple form and no complicated analysis. Anyone with a little intelligence and a book of instructions can handle the matter without outside help.

But there is always the chance that complications are involved that only an attorney would notice. To simplify the law into a book like this, several legal cases often must be condensed into a single sentence or paragraph. Otherwise, the book would be several hundred pages long and too complicated for most people. However, this simplification necessarily leaves out many details and nuances that would apply to special or unusual situations. Also, there are many ways to interpret most legal questions. Your case may come before a judge who disagrees with the analysis of our authors.

Therefore, in deciding to use a self-help law book and to do your own legal work, you must realize that you are making a cost/value analysis. You have decided that the money you will save in doing it yourself outweighs the chance that your case will not turn out to your satisfaction. Most people handling their own simple legal matters never have a problem, but occasionally people find that it ended up costing them more to have an attorney straighten out the situation than it would have if they had hired an attorney in the beginning. Keep this in mind if you decide to handle your own case, and be sure to consult an attorney if you feel you might need further guidance.

**Local Rules**

The next thing to remember is that a book that covers the law for the entire nation, or even for an entire state, cannot possibly include every procedural difference of every county court. Whenever possible, we provide the exact form needed; however, in some areas, each county, or even each judge, may require unique forms and procedures. In our *state* books, our forms usually cover the majority of counties in the state, or provide examples of the type of form that will be required. In our *national* books, our forms are sometimes even more general in nature but are designed to give a good idea of the type of form that will be needed in most locations. Nonetheless, keep in mind that your *state*, county, or judge may have a requirement, or use a form, that is not included in this book.

You should not necessarily expect to be able to get all of the information and resources you need solely from within the pages of this book. This book will serve as your guide, giving you specific information whenever possible and helping you to find out what else you will need to know. This is just like if you decided to build your own backyard deck. You might purchase a book on how to build decks. However, such a book would not include the building codes and permit requirements of every city, town, county, and township in the nation; nor would it include the lumber, nails, saws, hammers, and other materials and tools you would need to actually build the deck. You would use the book as your guide, and then do some work and research involving such matters as whether you need a permit of some kind, what type and grade of wood are available in your area, whether to use hand tools or power tools, and how to use those tools.

Before using the forms in a book like this, you should check with your court clerk to see if there are any local rules of which you should be aware, or local forms you will need to use. Often, such forms will require the same information as the forms in the book but are merely laid out differently, use slightly different language, or use different color paper so the clerks can easily find them. They will sometimes require additional information.

**Changes in the Law**

Besides being subject to state and local rules and practices, the law is subject to change at any time. The courts and the legislatures of all fifty states are constantly revising the laws. It is possible that while you are reading this book, some aspect of the law is being changed or a court is interpreting a law in a different way. You should always check the most recent statutes, rules and regulations to see what, if any changes have been made.

In most cases, the change will be of minimal significance. A form will be redesigned, additional information will be required, or a waiting period will be extended. As a result, you might need to revise a form, file an extra form, or wait out a longer time period; these types of changes will not usually affect the outcome of your case. On the other hand, sometimes a major part of the law is changed, the entire law in a particular area is rewritten, or a case that was the basis of a central legal point is overruled. In such instances, your entire ability to pursue your case may be impaired.

Again, you should weigh the value of your case against the cost of an attorney and make a decision as to what you believe is in your best interest.

# INTRODUCTION

This book is designed to enable you to form a general partnership without hiring a lawyer. Even if you do hire a lawyer, this book will help you to work with him or her more effectively. This can reduce your legal fees. This is not a law school course, but a practical guide to get your partnership going as easily as possible. Legal jargon has been kept to a minimum.

The old saying that knowledge is power is especially true in the law. This book will give you a fair amount of knowledge. By reading this book you will be able to know as much, or more, about partnerships as many recent law school graduates. By deciding to become your own lawyer, you are becoming responsible for your future. If you want to save money, you should use this book and do a little additional reading and research (which will be discussed later).

The difficulty in covering any area of the law on a multistate scale is that the law is different in each state. However, except in Louisiana, all states have adopted one of two basic set of laws regarding partnerships. This is one area of the law that is fairly uniform in most states.

Since the *Uniform Partnership Act* (UPA) or the *Revised Uniform Partnership Act* (RUPA) is the law in all states except Louisiana, they will be used as examples.

This book will give you an overview of partnership law; help you decide if you want to form a partnership; and, if you want to use an attorney, will guide you in preparing your **PARTNERSHIP AGREEMENT**. Appendix A contains a reference guide to the partnership laws of each state. Appendix B gives the text of the UPA, the RUPA, and the *Louisiana Partnership Act*.

Appendix C contains six basic partnership forms, three of which are partnership agreements. One is a very basic, simple form, for use by two partners in a fairly small and simple business. The second is a more comprehensive form. The last is specifically designed for an investment club. Appendix C also contains forms for transferring an interest in a partnership, adding new partners, changing a **PARTNERSHIP AGREEMENT**, and terminating a partnership.

These standardized forms may not fit your needs. In such a case, you can prepare your own custom **PARTNERSHIP AGREEMENT** by selecting from various paragraphs, or *clauses*, found in Appendix D.

None of these forms or clauses are rigidly required in any state. You are free to design your agreement to fit the needs of you and your partners. This means you can change the way the paragraphs or clauses read, and add new paragraphs or clauses that you create. By reading the various forms and clauses in this book, you will be able to craft your own partnership agreement.

Read this entire book before you prepare your **PARTNERSHIP AGREEMENT**. You may also want to visit your local library or law library to get more information. Chapter 3 will help you with this additional research. To complete the necessary forms, use the general instructions in the main part of this book. Review the information in the appendices and use the information from any additional reading and research you may do.

# I | OVERVIEW OF BUSINESSES AND PARTNERSHIPS

This chapter will explain various types of business organizations and help you decide if a partnership is the right form for your business.

## Types of Business Organizations

A *partnership* is only one type of business organization. There are basically five types of business organizations:

1. sole proprietorship;

2. partnership;

3. limited partnership;

4. corporation; and,

5. limited liability company.

Each of these has advantages and disadvantages and are discussed in the remaining pages.

**Sole
Proprietorship**

A *sole proprietorship* is simply a business owned by one person, as an individual. The main advantages to a sole proprietorship are that you are your own boss with no one to account to and it is the most simple form of business with respect to taxes and other government intervention. You pay taxes on your profit and file a *Schedule C* form with your regular personal income tax return.

**Partnership**

A *partnership* is a business owned by two or more people, who share in the profits or losses. A legal definition of a partnership is: a voluntary association of two or more persons to carry on, as co-owners, a business for profit.

**Limited
Partnership**

A *limited partnership* is a special kind of partnership, in which there are two classes of partners. One class is that of *general partners*. The general partners run the business and share in any profits or losses the same as in a regular partnership. The other class is that of *limited partners*. Limited partners contribute money, but are not allowed a say in how the business is operated. They might also be called *silent* partners. Usually, limited partners are only liable for losses up to the amount of money they contributed to the partnership.

> **Example:** Suppose there are two general partners and three limited partners. Each of the five people put in $2,000, for a total of $10,000. If the partnership loses $20,000, only the two general partners are responsible to pay that loss over the amount of the contributions from the limited partners.

However, some limited partnership agreements also require limited partners to contribute additional money under certain circumstances.

**Corporation**

A *corporation* is a business entity where one or more persons are owners of the business, by being owners of *stock* in the corporation. Legally speaking, the corporation is an entity of its own and is considered as a separate *person*. The corporation is separate from its individual stockholders. If the corporation loses money, only the corporation is responsible for paying the losses. The stockholders are not liable for losses.

More differences between these types of business organizations are discussed in the following sections of this chapter.

**Limited Liability
Company**

The *limited liability company* is designed to give the owners (called *members*) the limited liability of a corporation, while retaining at least some of the tax benefits of a partnership. None of the members have personal liability and all have some control of the business.

# Advantages of Partnerships

Depending on your need, setting up a partnership can have many advantages over other business entities.

**Compared to Sole Proprietorship**

The main advantage a partnership has over a sole proprietorship is that you will have the availability of the *assistance* of your partner or partners. Partners can assist you with such things as money, expertise, and the workload. For some people, being in business alone can be lonely and hard on the nerves. It can be nice to have someone to share the responsibilities and decision-making.

**Compared to Limited Partnership**

The primary advantage a partnership has over a *limited partnership* is that a partnership is usually more *simple*. For one thing, the partnership agreement is less complicated. For another, limited partnerships often get into more government regulation. Limited partnerships are generally required to:

✪  register with a state agency;

✪  pay an annual registration fee;

✪  have more complex tax requirements; and,

✪  may also come under federal and state securities regulations.

**Compared to Corporation**

The main advantage a partnership has over a corporation is in the areas of *taxes* and *government intervention*. A corporation must pay taxes on its profit. If any of that profit is then paid to stockholders as dividends, the stockholders then pay tax on the amount they receive. In such a case the profit of the corporation is taxed twice. (For small corporations, there is a way to get around this *double taxation* as far as the federal tax is concerned.) Additionally, in some states with no personal income tax, there is still an income tax on corporations.

Also, in order to incorporate, you must file an application with the state government. This application must generally be *renewed* each year. This can be expensive, as most states charge a fee for applications and annual renewals.

**Compared to
Limited Liability
Company**

As with the limited partnership and the corporation, the *limited liability* company is also more complex. Registration, along with an annual fee that may be higher than for a corporation, is typically required. Also, state corporate income taxes may need to be paid.

# Disadvantages of Partnerships

**Compared to
Sole
Proprietorship**

An advantage of a partnership over a sole proprietorship can *also be a disadvantage*. That partner who was initially nice to have around to help make decisions can quickly turn into someone to argue with over how the business should be run. In a partnership you do not always get your way. But in a sole proprietorship, you get to make all of the decisions. Only you are responsible for success or failure.

**Compared to
other Forms of
Business**

The main disadvantage of a partnership in comparison to a limited partnership, corporation, or limited liability company is the *unlimited liability* of a partnership. In a regular partnership, each partner is personally liable for the debts of the partnership. If your partner runs up a lot of debts for the business, or if the business loses a lawsuit, the creditors can come after your personal belongings to get paid (such as your personal bank accounts, car, boat, etc.). However, if your business is incorporated or registered as a limited liability company, the creditors can only come after money and property belonging to the business.

Similarly, if you are a limited partner in a limited partnership, creditors can only come after property of the business or the general partners. Your personal property is safe in such circumstances.

The idea of the business entities with limited liability of the owners came about as a way for the government to encourage people to start businesses to boost the economy. It is a way to go into business without risking everything you own.

Another possible advantage to other forms of doing business is in the area of taxes. Determining which type of business entity provides the best tax situation will depend upon many variables of the particular business in which you are involved. This can best be determined by a CPA or tax attorney.

# Deciding What is Best for You

First, take another look at the advantages and disadvantages of the various types of business organizations.

| Type of Organization | Limited Liability | Double Taxation | Government Regulation |
|---|---|---|---|
| Sole Proprietorship | No | No | Minimal |
| Partnership | No | No | Minimal |
| Limited Partnership | For limited partners | No | Moderate |
| Corporation | Yes | Maybe | Heavy |
| Limited Liability Company | Yes | Maybe | Varies by state |

How do you sort through all of this to determine which is best for your situation? If you have a lot of personal assets that you do not want to risk losing, you should probably incorporate. This is especially true if you will be engaging in a business that is more likely than others to subject you to lawsuits (such as a fireworks display business). It will be worth the extra taxes, expenses, government intervention, and paperwork hassle to protect your assets. On the other hand, if you are starting your business on a shoestring budget and do not have a lot of assets to protect, a sole proprietorship is probably the best choice.

A sole proprietorship is usually preferable to a partnership. A partnership should usually be your last choice. It seems to be human nature for partners to argue, whether they are partners in business or partners in marriage. Partnerships, like borrowing money, have destroyed countless friendships.

Generally, you should only take on a partner if you absolutely need that person's money or expertise. First, you may want to see if you can get the money as a loan or hire the person as an employee or consultant to get the expertise. This way you will not be giving up control of your business. A partnership is essentially a business run by a democracy.

Before you commit yourself to taking on a partner, consider what may happen if you disagree. There will be times when a decision must be made that will determine the success or failure of your business. What are you going to do when you and your partner disagree on this decision?

***Example:*** Suppose that about a year after you start your business, the nation's economy goes into recession. Your income drops drastically. You decide that it is necessary to increase spending on advertising in order to reach the customers that are still in a buying mood (this is a commonly accepted and recommended course of action in the business world). Your partner insists that you must cut spending in all areas, especially advertising. What will you do?

If you decide to take on a partner, it is important to choose your partner carefully and to prepare a good **PARTNERSHIP AGREEMENT**. (see form 1 and form 2, pages 125 and 127.) This can help reduce friction between the partners by clearly defining what each partner's role is in operating the business. One of the most vital parts of the agreement is to agree on how to settle disagreements. However, no **PARTNERSHIP AGREEMENT** can totally prevent friction between partners. This is why it is important to choose the right partner and to consider such things as your respective personalities, comfort with risk, goals, philosophy of life, etc.

***Example:*** If you are a workaholic and your partner does not believe in working weekends, you may begin to feel that you are doing all of the work. You may become resentful of your partner.

Before we get into the details of a **PARTNERSHIP AGREEMENT,** we will look at the law that governs partnerships, as well as your proposed partner or partners.

# 2 | LAWYERS

This chapter will help you determine if you want to hire a lawyer to help you form your partnership. If you decide that you do want a lawyer, this chapter will also give you tips on selecting a lawyer, evaluating a lawyer, and on working with a lawyer. We will also discuss firing your lawyer in the event you become unsatisfied with his or her services.

## Needing a Lawyer

Do you need a lawyer? The answer to this question will depend upon whom you ask. If you ask a lawyer, he or she will probably say that you definitely need one. However, by the time you are finished reading this book, you will know almost as much as most lawyers about partnerships, including how to write a **PARTNERSHIP AGREEMENT**.

The purpose of a **PARTNERSHIP AGREEMENT** is to avoid potential problems, so your agreement needs to cover the possible problem areas. The way most lawyers would approach this would be to consult a book such as this, look at examples of other partnership agreements (that either he or she has done for others or other lawyers have prepared), and put together various clauses or paragraphs to fit your situation. That is exactly what this book will enable you to do for yourself.

One of the first questions you may have about a lawyer, and most likely the reason you are reading this book, is—"How much will an attorney cost?" Attorneys come in all ages, shapes, sizes, sexes, racial and ethnic groups—and price ranges. For a very rough estimate, you can probably expect an attorney to charge anywhere from $150 to $750 for a partnership agreement. Of course, these fees may vary from state to state.

If you need complicated business or tax advice, you may need to see a tax lawyer or CPA. If large sums of money are at stake or you want to tie your partnership into your estate planning, you may need to see a lawyer. If you decide to hire a lawyer, the remainder of this chapter will help you to select and work with him or her more effectively.

# Selecting a Lawyer

Selecting a lawyer is a two-step process. First you need to decide which attorney to make an appointment with, then you need to decide if you want to hire that attorney.

The following are suggestions that may help you to find a lawyer for further consideration.

***Ask a Friend***  A common, and frequently the best, way to find a lawyer is to ask someone you know to recommend one. This is especially helpful if the lawyer handled a business matter for your friend.

***Lawyer Referral Service***  You can find an attorney through a lawyer referral service by looking in the Yellow Pages phone directory under "Attorney Referral Services" or "Attorneys." This is a service, usually operated by a bar association. It is designed to match a client with an attorney handling cases in the area of law the client needs. Typically, a referral service operated by the state or local bar association does not guarantee the quality of work, the level of experience, or the ability of the attorney. In some areas there are private referral services that do provide certain guarantees of quality and satisfaction. Finding a lawyer this way will at least connect you with one who is interested in business law matters, and one who probably has some experience in this area.

**Yellow Pages**    Check under the heading for "Attorneys" in the Yellow Pages. Many of the lawyers and law firms will place display ads here indicating their areas of practice and educational backgrounds. Look for firms or lawyers that indicate they practice in areas such as *Partnerships*, *Corporations*, *Business Law*, *Contracts*, *Commercial Transactions*, or *Business Litigation*.

**Ask Another Lawyer**    If you have used the services of an attorney in the past for some other matter (for example, a real estate closing, traffic ticket, or a will), you may want to call and ask if he or she handles partnership agreements, or could refer you to an attorney whose ability in that area is respected.

# Evaluating a Lawyer

From your search you should select three to five lawyers worthy of further consideration. Your first step will be to call each attorney's office, explain that you are interested in having a partnership agreement prepared, and ask the following questions.

✪    Does the attorney (or firm) handle preparation of partnership agreements?

✪    How much can you expect it to cost?

✪    How soon can you get an appointment?

If you like the answers you get, ask if you can speak to the attorney. Some offices will permit this, but others will require you to make an appointment. Make the appointment if that is what is required. Once you get in contact with the attorney (either on the phone or at the appointment), ask the following questions.

✪    How much will it cost and how will the fee be paid?

✪    How long has the attorney been in practice?

✪    Has the attorney prepared many partnership agreements or handled much partnership litigation?

✪    Approximately what portion of the attorney's business relates to business law matters? (The answer should be 25% or more.)

✪     How long will it take to get an agreement prepared?

If you get acceptable answers to these questions, it's time to ask yourself the following questions about the lawyer.

✪     Do you feel comfortable talking to the lawyer?

✪     Is the lawyer friendly toward you?

✪     Does the lawyer seem confident in himself or herself?

✪     Does the lawyer seem to be straight-forward with you, and able to explain things so you understand?

If you get satisfactory answers to all of these questions, you probably have a lawyer you will be able to work with. Most clients are happiest using an attorney with whom they feel comfortable.

# Working with a Lawyer

In general, you will work best with your attorney if you keep an open, honest, and friendly attitude. You should also consider the following suggestions.

*Ask Questions*     If you want to know something or if you do not understand something, ask your attorney. If you do not understand the answer, tell your attorney and ask him or her to explain it again. There are points of law that many lawyers do not fully understand, so you should not be embarrassed to ask questions. Many people who say they had a bad experience with a lawyer either did not ask enough questions or had a lawyer who wouldn't take the time to explain things to them. If your lawyer is not taking the time to explain what he's doing, it may be time to look for a new lawyer.

*Give Complete Information*     Anything you tell your attorney is confidential. An attorney can lose his or her license to practice if he or she reveals information without your permission. So do not hold back information.

*Accept Reality*     Listen to what your lawyer tells you about the law and the legal system—and accept it. It will do you no good to argue because the law or the system does not work the way you think it should. It is not your attorney's fault that the system is not perfect, or that the law does not say what you would like it to say.

**Be Patient**

Do not expect your lawyer to return your phone call within an hour. He or she may not be able to return it the same day either. Most lawyers are very busy and overworked. It is rare that an attorney can maintain a full caseload and still make each client feel as if he or she is the only client.

**Talk to the Secretary**

Your lawyer's secretary can be a valuable source of information. So be friendly and get to know the secretary. Often he or she will be able to answer your questions and you won't get a bill for the time you talk to him or her.

**Keep Your Case Moving**

Many lawyers operate on the old principle of *the squeaking wheel gets the oil*. Work on a case tends to get put off until a deadline is near, an emergency develops, or the client calls. This is because many lawyers take more cases than can be effectively handled in order to make the income they desire. Your task is to become a squeaking wheel that doesn't squeak so much that the lawyer wants to avoid you. Whenever you talk to your lawyer ask the following questions.

✪    What is the next step?

✪    When do you expect it to be done?

✪    When should I talk to you next?

**Save Money**

If you do not hear from the lawyer when you expect, call him or her the following day. Do not remind him or her of the missed call—just ask how things are going.

Of course, you do not want to spend unnecessary money for an attorney. Here are a few things you can do to avoid excess legal fees.

✪    Do not make unnecessary phone calls to your lawyer.

✪    Give information to the secretary whenever possible.

✪    Direct your question to the secretary first. He or she will refer it to the attorney if he or she cannot answer it.

✪ Plan your phone calls so you can get to the point and take less of your attorney's time. Write down an outline if necessary.

✪ Do some of the *leg work* yourself. Pick up and deliver papers yourself, for example. Ask your attorney what you can do to assist with your case.

✪ Be prepared for appointments. Have all related papers with you. Plan your visit to get to the point. Make an outline of what you want to discuss and what questions you want to ask.

**Pay Your Attorney Bill on Time**

No client gets more prompt attention than the client who pays the bill on time. However, you are entitled to an itemized bill, showing what the attorney did and how much time it took. If your attorney asks for money in advance, you should be sure that you and the lawyer agree on what is to be done for this fee.

# Firing Your Lawyer

If you find that you can no longer work with your lawyer or do not trust your lawyer, it is time to either go it alone or get a new attorney. You will need to send your lawyer a letter stating that you no longer desire his or her services, and are discharging him or her from your case. Also state that you will be coming by the office the following day to pick up your file. The attorney does not have to give you his or her own notes or other work in progress, but the essential contents of your file (such as copies of papers already prepared and billed for, and any documents you provided) must be given to you. If the lawyer refuses to give you your file, for any reason, contact your state's bar association about filing a complaint or *grievance*. Of course, you will need to settle any remaining fees owed.

# 3 | PARTNERSHIP LAW

This chapter will explain the basic legal principals regarding partnerships. It will include general principals that are fairly uniformly applied in all states; how to find the law for your particular state; state and federal tax information; and, legal considerations in choosing your partnership name.

## Partnership Law in General

All states, except Louisiana, have adopted what is called the *Uniform Partnership Act* (commonly referred to as the UPA). (Louisiana's partnership law is not much different.) In the past several years, some states have adopted the *Revised Uniform Partnership Act* (RUPA). It is designed as an improvement over the original UPA. The UPA and RUPA were written by a group of lawyers with the idea of standardizing the laws regarding partnerships throughout the United States. The basic UPA and RUPA may be found in Appendix B of this book, although there may be slight variations in your state. Such variations will be discussed further in the following sections of this chapter. The *Louisiana Partnership Act* may also be found in Appendix B.

The UPA and RUPA define the basic legal rights and obligations of partnerships and their partners. Some, but not all, of these basic rights and obligations can be changed by a **PARTNERSHIP AGREEMENT**. (See form 1 and form 2, pages 125 and 127.) The following information about the law is based on the UPA and RUPA. Many of these are general rules of law that apply unless your **PARTNERSHIP AGREEMENT** provides for something different. On some matters, however, the law cannot be changed by a **PARTNERSHIP AGREEMENT**. These matters usually relate to dealings with third parties, not to dealings between the partners.

> *Warning:* The discussion of the law in this chapter is of a general nature only and should not be relied upon in preparing an agreement or in operating your partnership business. In order to fully understand the law it is strongly suggested that you take the time to read your state's partnership act.

Partnership laws basically cover the following areas:

- ✪ definition of terms;

- ✪ when a partnership exists;

- ✪ registration of the partnership with a state agency;

- ✪ the relationship of the partners with each other;

- ✪ the relationship between the partnership and third parties; and,

- ✪ changing and terminating the partnership.

**When a Partnership Exists**

A partnership is an association of two or more persons to carry on a business for profit as *co-owners*. Of course, if these people take the necessary legal steps to form a limited partnership, corporation, or limited liability company, then they do not have a partnership. Refer to the partnership acts in Appendix B and your state's partnership law, for more information about what does, or does not, make a person a partner in a partnership.

**Relationship of Partners**

The relationship of the partners includes matters such as decision-making; how property is titled and transferred; how a partner may sell his or her interest in the business; how new partners may join the partnership; what happens if a partner dies; how the partnership may be ended; and, what a partner may or may not do without the agreement of the other partners. This last matter overlaps on the subject of the relationship of the partnership to third parties with whom the partnership conducts its business. (See Chapter 4, the partnership acts in Appendix B, and your state's partnership law, for more information.)

**Relationship of Partnership to Third Parties**

As a co-owner, each partner has the authority to act for the partnership. Each is responsible for the acts of the other partners. This means that your partner can enter into contracts, open bank accounts, buy and sell partnership property, create partnership debts, file lawsuits, and generally conduct business for the partnership.

You, as a partner, will be *personally obligated* for the actions of your partners the same as if you had done them yourself. To be personally obligated means that your personal possessions (such as your bank accounts, house, car, etc.) may be taken to satisfy the obligations.

**Example:** Suppose you have a wholesale ping pong table manufacturing business. Your partner buys on credit a large amount of plywood from a supplier, which is used to make ping pong tables for a department store chain. Sales to the department store chain are 80% of your business.

The department store chain sells most of your tables, uses the money to pay its employees, and then declares bankruptcy. You do not get paid, so you cannot pay your plywood supplier. The plywood supplier sues your business, but your business does not have enough money or other property to satisfy the debt. After taking the partnership's bank accounts and other property, the plywood supplier can come after your personal bank accounts, boat, second car, etc.

There are some limits on what can be done without the agreement of all of the partners. Third parties are assumed to know these limits (so you will not be liable if a partner acts alone in one of these matters). The agreement of all of the partners is required, unless the **PARTNERSHIP AGREEMENT** provides otherwise, to do any of the following:

- ✪ assign partnership property in trust for a creditor;
- ✪ assign partnership property to someone in return for that person's promise to pay debts of the partnership;

✪   sell or transfer the goodwill of the business;

✪   do anything that would make it impossible to carry on normal business;

✪   confess a judgment (this means admitting to liability in a lawsuit); or,

✪   submit a partnership claim or liability to arbitration.

Also, no partner can act in violation of a restriction on his or her authority. If such a restriction is violated, the partnership is not liable for the act as to third persons who know about the restriction.

More about the law of partnerships will be discussed in later chapters of this book.

# The Law in Your State

All states, except Louisiana, have adopted the UPA or RUPA, although some states have made slight changes. Appendix B contains the basic UPA, RUPA, and the Louisiana Partnership Act. Your state may have rearranged the order of the sections without changing the substance of the Act. Your state may have also changed a few more significant provisions, which you can only find out by reading your state's version of the UPA or RUPA.

Appendix A will tell you where to find your state's partnership laws so you can look them up for yourself. There is also a set of books called *Uniform Laws Annotated*, which tells how each state has modified the basic UPA or RUPA.

The listing for your state in Appendix A will give you some basic information about the law in your state. While every effort is made to assure that the most recent information available is incorporated in this book, the law may change at any time. This is especially true in the area of partnerships, as there is a trend for states to replace the UPA with the RUPA. Therefore, it is suggested that you read the most current version of your state's partnership laws. This can usually be done by visiting your local library or online.

If your public library does not have the most current version of your state's laws, you may need to visit a law library. More information about checking the most current version of the law is provided in the section of this Chapter titled "Legal Research" and at the beginning of Appendix A.

# Taxes

You will need a tax advisor for your partnership business. This should be either a CPA or a tax attorney who has significant experience with small businesses. Tax problems can destroy a business, so you need someone who is knowledgeable and keeps up to date with the changes in the tax code. This section will give you some basic ideas regarding taxes, but it will not substitute for a tax professional.

***Federal Taxes***

For federal income tax purposes, you will pay taxes on your share of the profits of the partnership. This will be reported on an IRS Form 1065. The partnership itself is not taxed. Instead, the distributed partnership income of each partner is taxed to that partner. The partnership will need to file a partnership tax return for *informational purposes*, but no tax will be paid. Each partner will report his or her share of the distributed income on his or her individual tax return, and pay any tax that may be due. Quarterly tax returns will also need to be filed by each partner. Exactly what is considered *distributed* to each partner is a matter of tax law and IRS rules. It may even include money kept by the partnership after all expenses are paid.

There can also be tax consequences for the following matters:

✪ noncash property contributions to the partnership;

✪ contributions of services;

✪ expenses incurred before the partnership agreement is signed;

✪ various other transactions between the partnership and an individual partner or between two or more partners;

✪ the sale of a partnership interest;

✪ the death or retirement of a partner; or,

✪ termination of the partnership.

**State Taxes**    There may also be state tax laws to deal with. These can include such things as income taxes, inventory taxes, sales or excise taxes, and license and filing fees.

**The Bottom Line**    The bottom line is that you would be well advised to consult a tax expert if you want to go into business as a partnership. Even if you would feel comfortable doing your own taxes as a sole proprietorship, there are several reasons that you might not want to do so as a partnership. Although a partnership itself is not taxed and the profits are passed on to the individual partners, there are additional tax forms that must be prepared and filed. Additional calculations must be made to properly allocate the profit or loss between the partners so that they can file their personal tax returns. This can be made more complicated if property is being depreciated.

If you are the one doing the tax forms for the partnership, you are taking on the responsibility for providing the correct information to your partner. In the opposite situation, are you willing to trust your partner to, in essence, be your tax advisor and provide you with accurate tax information? Mistakes can be costly and interest charges and penalties can be so high that they run you out of business. Further, partners are personally liable for partnership debts. Because partnership profits and losses are attributable to the individual partners, the IRS may go after you personal property as well as partnership property.

# Partnership Name

In addition to marketing and advertising considerations, there are a few legal issues to consider in choosing a name for your partnership.

**Conducting Business and Title to Property**    To identify your business you will either use the names of the partners (e.g., Smith, Jones, and Johnson), or a business name (e.g., Tri-County Furniture). Traditionally, the business of the partnership had to be conducted in the names of all of the partners. Title to any property was held by the partners in their names. Today, however, under the partnership laws of all fifty states and the District of Columbia, a business name may be used and title to property may be held in the name of the business.

**Fictitious Name Registration**    In most locations, if you use a business name it will need to be registered with a local or state agency. This is frequently referred to as a *fictitious* or *assumed* name. The purpose of this type of registration is to allow those with whom your partnership does business to know who the partners are. Generally this does not protect your business name. You may find there is someone else in your area using the same name for his or her business.

**Partnership Registration**

Some states also allow, or require, a partnership to register with a state agency, in much the same manner as a corporation. Depending upon state law, this may or may not offer protection against others using the name. In many states, such registration is primarily a way for the state to generate additional revenue, while providing little if any advantage to the partnership.

**NOTE:** *If you want to be sure to protect your business name, you should consider state or federal trade name registration.*

# Legal Research

Appendix A of this book provides some information regarding the law in each state. It will give you a starting point for looking further.

While every effort is made to assure that the most recent information available is incorporated in this book, the law may change at any time. Therefore, it is advisable to check on the most current version of your state's laws before preparing and executing any forms. This can usually be done by visiting your local public library or online.

If your public library does not have the most current version of your state's laws, you may need to visit a law library. Law libraries can usually be found at or near your local county courthouse, or at a law school. Ask the librarian to help you find what you need. The law librarian cannot give you legal advice, but can show you where to find your state's laws and other materials on partnerships. Some typical sources are discussed in the following subsections.

**Statutes or Code**

The main source of information will be the set of volumes that contain the laws passed by your state legislature. Unless you are extremely curious about details of the partnership law, this is generally as far as you need to go. Depending upon your state, these will be referred to as either the *statutes* or the *code* of your state.

**Example:** *Florida Statutes* or *Mississippi Code*.

The actual title of the books may also include words such as *Revised* or *Annotated*.

**Example:** *Annotated California Code, Illinois Statutes Annotated, Kentucky Revised Statutes*, or *Maine Revised Statutes Annotated*.

The word *revised* simply means updated. The word *annotated* means that the books contain summaries of court decisions and other information that explain and interpret the laws.

In some states, the titles will also include the name of the publisher, such as *West's Colorado Revised Statutes Annotated, Vernon's Annotated Missouri Statutes*, or *Purdon's Pennsylvania Consolidated Statutes Annotated*. The listing for your state in Appendix A gives the title of the set of laws for your state. A few states have more than one set of books, by various publishers.

**Example:** Florida has both *Florida Statutes* and *Florida Statutes Annotated*.

Each state's listing in Appendix A will give the name of the set of books used by this author. Ask the law librarian for help if you have any problems in locating your state's partnership laws.

*Supplements.* Each year the legislature meets and changes the law, therefore, it is important to be sure you have the most current version. Once you locate the set of books at the library, you will find that they are updated in one of three ways. The most common way to update laws is with a soft-cover supplement (called a *pocket part*), which will be found in the back of each volume. There will be a date on the cover of the supplement to tell you when it was published (such as *2002 Cumulative Supplement*). If it is more than one year old, ask the librarian if it is the most current supplement.

Another way laws are updated is with a supplement volume, which will be found at the end of the regular set of volumes. This will also have a date or year on it. A few states also use a looseleaf binding, in which pages are removed and replaced, or a supplement section added, as the law changes.

**Online Research**    The statutes of most states and other legal information can be accessed online through **www.findlaw.com**. Once you get to the site, click on "US State Resources," then click on the name of the state you want, then click on "Primary Materials – Cases, Codes and Regulations," then click on the name of the state code or statutes. Findlaw will also give you links to state and federal court opinions, state and federal agencies, and numerous other legal resources.

If you want to skip navigating through the Findlaw site, you can go straight to your state's website (found in the listing for your state in Appendix A). These are the current state websites at the time of publication, however, they may change at any time. If you have any problem with the state website, you can always go through the Findlaw website.

**Uniform Laws Annotated**

The *Uniform Laws Annotated* is a set of books containing all of the various uniform laws, such as the Uniform Partnership Act, Uniform Probate Act, Uniform Commercial Code, etc. This will give you the text of the uniform act; tell you which states have adopted it; and, whether each state has changed it in any way.

**Practice Manuals**

*Practice manuals* are books written for lawyers that give detailed, practical information on various areas of the law. At the law library you should be able to find such books about partnership law in your state, including sample forms. Some of these books are written in connection with seminars for lawyers and they can be very helpful in answering your questions about very specific situations.

**Case Law**

You probably will not need to do any more research than to look up the partnership law provisions in your state's statutes or code, and look at some of the forms in a form and practice manual. However, just in case you want to go further with your research, the following information is provided. In addition to the laws passed by the legislature, law is also made by the decisions of the judges in various cases each year. These decisions will explain and interpret the law found in the statutes or code, but only in the context of a lawsuit. To find this *case law* you will need to go to a law library. In addition to annotated codes or statutes, there are several types of books used to find the case law, discussed next.

*Digests.* A *digest* is a set of volumes that gives short summaries of appellate court cases and tells you where you can find the court's full written opinion. The information in the digest is arranged alphabetically by subject. First, try to find a digest for your state (such as *New York Digest*). There is a *General Digest* that covers the entire United States, but it will be easier to find your state's cases in a state digest. Look for the chapter on "Partnerships," then look for the headings for the subject you want. If you can't find a chapter titled "Partnerships," look in the index under "Partnerships" to find out what chapter title you should use.

***Case Reporters.*** *Case reporters* are numerous volumes of books where appellate courts publish their written opinions on the cases they hear. There may be a specific reporter for your state or you may need to use a regional reporter which contains cases from several states in your area. Your librarian can help you locate the reporter for your state. There may be two (or even three) *series* of the regional reporter, the second series being newer than the first.

**Example:** If the digest refers you to "*Smith v. National Manufacturing*, 149 So.2d 721 (1986)," this indicates that you can find the case titled *Smith v. National Manufacturing* by going to Volume 149 (the first number listed) of the *Southern Reporter 2d Series*, and turning to page 721 (the second number listed). The number in parentheses (1986) is the year the court decided the case.

In its opinion, the court will discuss what the case was about, what questions of law were presented for consideration, and what the court decided and why.

***Legal Encyclopedia.*** A *legal encyclopedia* is similar to a regular encyclopedia. You simply look up the subject you want (such as "Partnerships"), in alphabetical order, and it gives you a summary of the law on that subject. It will also refer to specific court cases that can then be found in the Reporter. On a national level, the two main sets are *American Jurisprudence* (abbreviated Am. Jur.), and *Corpus Juris Secundum* (C.J.S.). You may also find a set for your state, such as *Florida Jurisprudence*. Ask the law librarian to show you where the legal encyclopedia for your state is located.

# 4 | YOUR PARTNERS

You cannot be too careful when choosing business partners. This is almost as important as choosing a husband or wife. When you take on a business partner, you are allowing that person to represent you, so it had better be a person you can trust not to get you into trouble. This chapter looks at what a partner can and cannot do.

## Authority of a Partner

Generally, each partner has the authority to act for the partnership. What one partner does in the name of the partnership will be binding on all of the other partners. If your partner signs a contract on behalf of the partnership, you will be obligated to comply with the terms of that contract. Your partner does not need to get your agreement or even tell you about it.

**Limitations on Authority by Law**

There are two ways in which a partner's authority is limited. The first way is by the *Uniform Partnership Act* itself. The Act says that it takes the agreement of all of the partners to:

✪   assign partnership property in trust for a creditor;

✪   assign partnership property to someone in return for that person's promise to pay debts of the partnership;

✪   sell or transfer the goodwill of the business;

✪   do anything that would make it impossible to carry on normal business;

✪   confess a judgment (this means admitting to liability in a lawsuit); or,

✪   submit a partnership claim or liability to arbitration.

**Limitations on Authority by Agreement**

The second way to limit a partner's authority is by the agreement of the partners. This is done by including a limitation in a **PARTNERSHIP AGREEMENT**. (see form 1 and form 2, pages 125 and 127.) No partner can act in violation of a restriction on his or her authority. If such a restriction is violated, the partnership is not liable for the act as to third persons who know about the restriction. However, if the third person does not know about the limitation, the partners are still obligated.

**Example:** Suppose that Wilbur Wright and Orville Wright are partners in a retail bicycle shop. They sign a partnership agreement that says both partners must agree to expand into a new line of products. Wilbur decides that they should expand into in-line skates and takes it upon himself to order 100 pairs of in-line skates from the FastBlades Company.

The FastBlades Company has never seen a copy of the Wrights' partnership agreement. It has no idea that Wilbur does not have the authority to place such an order. Therefore, the partnership (and Orville) is still obligated to pay for the skates. Orville can sue Wilbur for violating the partnership agreement, but this has no effect on the FastBlades Company.

The ideal situation, or as close to ideal as possible, is to have worked extensively with your intended partner. This way you will know each other's work habits and personalities and have a better idea of whether you can get along in a partnership.

# 5 WRITING A PARTNERSHIP AGREEMENT

This chapter will help guide you in preparing your own **PARTNERSHIP AGREEMENT**. Appendix C of this book contains a short form partnership agreement. (see form 1, p.125.) It also has a longer version. (see form 2, p.127.) You may also wish to create your own custom agreement by selecting various paragraphs to fit your situation from the clauses found in Appendix D. We will discuss each of these separately.

## Short Form Partnership Agreement

Form 1 in Appendix C is for those who want a short and simple agreement. This agreement leaves great freedom to make changes in the way the partnership operates. (see form 1, p.125.) It is written for two partners, although additional signature spaces may be added if needed. This agreement does not cover many items that would be included in a comprehensive agreement. Any of the paragraphs may be changed. You may want to look at the variations and additional clauses in Appendix D.

Form 1 should be completed as follows:

◈ Type in the date in the appropriate spaces in the first, unnumbered, paragraph.

◈ Type in the names of all of the persons who will be partners in the same paragraph.

◈ In paragraph 1, type in the name of the partnership and the name of the partnership business. These may be the same or different.

***Example:*** Fred and Barney decide to open a retail gourmet cheese business. They may want to call their partnership and the store *Fred & Barney's Gourmet Cheeses*. On the other hand, they may want to call their partnership *F & B Enterprises* and call the store *Fred & Barney's Gourmet Cheeses*.

◈ In paragraph 2, type in the street and mailing address for the partnership.

◈ In paragraph 3, type in a brief description of the type of business the partnership will conduct. This information is not absolutely essential, unless the agreement prohibits partners from going into a competing business venture, but it helps clearly define what the partners intend to do with their business. If you want a more broad ability to conduct business, you could add a provision stating—*In addition to the specific purpose set forth above, the purpose of the partnership is also to conduct any lawful business in which the partners, from time to time, may agree to become engaged.*

***Example:*** For Fred and Barney, they would type in something like: *to operate a retail gourmet cheese outlet.*

◈ Read paragraph 4. If you have other plans about terminating the partnership, refer to the alternative termination provisions in Appendix D.

◈ In paragraph 5, type in the amount of money each partner will contribute to starting up the business. If each partner is not contributing an equal amount of cash, refer to form 2, page 127, or the alternative contribution clauses in Appendix D.

◈ Read paragraph 6. If you have other plans for how profits and losses are to be shared, refer to the alternative profit and loss, and ownership interests provisions in Appendix D.

◈ Read paragraph 7. This paragraph requires that all decisions be made by the unanimous agreement of both partners. If you have more than one partner or if you have other plans about voting rights or how decisions should be made, refer to the alternative voting rights provisions in Appendix D.

◈ In paragraph 8.C., type in the missing terms for how payment is to be made. The provision in this form gives the partnership the easiest way to pay, by installment payments instead of having to come up with a lump sum of cash. See the alternative provisions in Appendix D for other ways of making payment.

◈ In paragraph 9, type in the name of your state.

◈ Paragraphs 10 through 13 are standard paragraphs that should be a part of all partnership agreements.

◈ Below paragraph 13 are lines for each partner to sign the agreement.

# Long Form Partnership Agreement

Form 2 in Appendix C, page 127, is a longer and more comprehensive **PARTNERSHIP AGREEMENT**. It has taken certain selected clauses from Appendix D and made modifications to some. If it does not fit your situation, you will need to create your own agreement from the clauses in Appendix D. In such a case, this form will be of help in showing you how it was crafted from the various clauses in Appendix D.

Form 2 should be completed as follows:

◈ Type in the date in the appropriate spaces in the first, unnumbered, paragraph.

➡️ Type in the names of all of the persons who will be partners in the same paragraph.

➡️ In paragraph 1, type in the name of the partnership and the name of the partnership business. These may be the same or different.

**Example:**    Fred and Barney decide to open a retail gourmet cheese business. They may want to call their partnership and the store *Fred & Barney's Gourmet Cheeses*. On the other hand, they may want to call their partnership *F & B Enterprises* and call the store *Fred & Barney's Gourmet Cheeses*.

➡️ In paragraph 2, type in the street and mailing address for the partnership.

➡️ In paragraph 3, type in a brief description of the type of business the partnership will conduct. This information is not absolutely essential, unless the agreement prohibits partners from going into a competing business venture, but it helps clearly define what the partners intend to do with their business. If you want a more broad ability to conduct business, you could add a provision stating—*In addition to the specific purpose set forth above, the purpose of the partnership is also to conduct any lawful business in which the partners, from time to time, may agree to become engaged.*

**Example:**    For Fred and Barney, they would type in something like: *to operate a retail gourmet cheese outlet.*

➡️ Read paragraph 4. If you have other plans about terminating the partnership, refer to the alternative termination provisions in Appendix D.

➡️ In paragraph 5, for each partner's contributions type in the name of the partner under the first column, the type of contribution (such as *Cash, 2004 GMC truck, Computer and software*, etc.) in the second column, and the amount of cash or value in the third column. Be sure to review the alternative contribution clauses in Appendix D to see if any are more appropriate for your situation.

➡️ In paragraph 6, type in the information for any loans being made to the business by any partners. The first column is for the name of the partner. The second column is for the amount to be loaned to the partnership. In the third column fill in the period of the loan, such as *6 months*, or *3 years*. The interest rate goes in the fourth column.

◈ In paragraph 7, fill in the information for any property being loaned to the partnership by any partners. The description of the property should be as specific as possible in order to avoid any confusion later about what was loaned.

◈ Read paragraph 8. If you have other plans for how additional contributions are to be handled, refer to the alternative additional contributions clauses in Appendix D.

◈ In paragraph 9, type in the name of each partner, and the percentage of the profits and losses that will be attributable to each partner. Make sure that the total percentages in each of the profits and losses columns add up to 100%. Also, read subparagraphs A and B. If you have other plans for how profits and losses are to be shared, refer to the alternative profit and loss and ownership interests provisions in Appendix D.

◈ In paragraph 10, type in the name of each partner, and the percentage of the partnership that is owned by each. Make sure the total percentages add up to 100%. If you have other plans for how ownership interests are to be determined, refer to the alternative ownership interests clauses in Appendix D.

◈ Read paragraph 11. This paragraph requires that all decisions be made by a majority vote of the partners. If you have other plans about voting rights or how decisions should be made, refer to the alternative voting rights clauses in Appendix D.

◈ In paragraph 12, type the name of each partner, and what each partner's job, duties, or role will be in running the partnership. In the second paragraph, type in the minimum number of hours each partner will work each week. After the word "Vacation," type in the number of vacation days each partner will be entitled to take per year. After the words "Sick Leave," type in the number of sick days each partner will be entitled to each year. After the word "Holidays," type in the names of the holidays when the business will be closed.

◈ Read paragraph 13. If you have other plans relating to salaries for partners, refer to the alternative salaries clauses in Appendix D.

◈ Read paragraphs 14 and 15. These are standard accounting clauses covering the maintenance of accounting records and accounting to the partners.

◈ In paragraph 16, fill in the number of partners you agree will be needed to sign checks or withdraw money from bank accounts.

◈ In paragraph 17, list the name of each partner who will receive an expense account, and the monthly maximum amount allowed for each account. If you have other plans relating to expense accounts, refer to the alternative expense account clauses in Appendix D.

◈ In paragraph 18, fill in the amount of life and disability insurance to be maintained on each partner in subparagraphs B and C.

◈ In paragraph 19, type in when the periodic partnership meetings will take place.

◈ In paragraph 20.D., type in the missing terms for how payment is to be made. The provision in this form gives the partnership the easiest way to pay, by installment payments instead of having to come up with a lump sum of cash. See the alternative provisions in Appendix D for other ways of making payment.

◈ In paragraph 21, fill in the number of days agreed upon as reasonable in items 4 and 5. Typically, 30, 60, or 90 days would be used.

◈ In paragraph 22, type in the business name of the partnership.

◈ In paragraph 24.A., type in the name of the person who by agreement will serve as mediator in the event of any disputes. This should not be a partner, or a member of any partner's family. Also fill in the number of days in the sentence regarding when mediation will commence.

◈ In paragraph 26, type in the name of your state.

◈ Paragraphs 27 through 30 are standard paragraphs which should be a part of all partnership agreements.

◈ Below paragraph 30 are lines for each partner to sign the agreement.

# Investment Club Partnership Agreement

There may be situations where you need a **PARTNERSHIP AGREEMENT** that is very specifically tailored to a particular type of operation. One such area that is becoming more and more popular is investment clubs. Therefore, we have included a **PARTNERSHIP AGREEMENT** (form 6, p.143) in Appendix C, that is specifically designed for such use.

To complete form 6:

◈ Type in the date in the appropriate spaces in the first unnumbered paragraph.

◈ Type in the names of all of the persons who will be partners in the same paragraph.

◈ In paragraph 1, type in the name of the partnership.

◈ In paragraph 2, type in the street and mailing address for the partnership. You may rotate your meetings between partners' residences, or meet at a restaurant, but you should select one partner's address for use as a mailing address when dealing with brokers and others.

◈ Paragraph 3 gives a description of the purpose of an investment club partnership.

◈ On the first line in paragraph 5, type in the amount of money each partner will contribute on a monthly basis. Generally, each of you will contribute a set amount each month to be invested. In addition to monthly investments, your club may also need a small amount of money for administrative expenses, such as to buy postage stamps, a file box, and notebooks for keeping records. The second line in this paragraph is to note how much will be contributed by each partner toward these expenses. If partners are simply going to contribute the necessary supplies, you can type in the number zero (-0-). You can add more if needed.

◈　In paragraph 16, type in when your meetings will be held, such as *first Tuesday* or *3rd day*.

◈　In paragraph 18, there are two spaces to fill in the percentage of a partner's capital account that is to be returned in the event of expulsion for various reasons. This could be 100%, but it is common to use a lesser amount as a penalty.

◈　In paragraph 20, type in the name of your state.

◈　On the last page are signature spaces for up to ten partners.

# Creating Your Own Partnership Agreement

If none of the **PARTNERSHIP AGREEMENT** forms in Appendix C can be made to fit your needs, you can use the clauses in Appendix D to create your own custom-made agreement. You will simply go through Appendix D page by page, and select the clauses you want to use in your agreement. You will then need to type up an agreement with the clauses you selected. You do not need to use every type of clause that you will find in Appendix D, although the more complete your agreement, the less room you leave for argument.

Be sure to read the previous two sections about form 1 and form 2, because they will help you understand how to fill in the blanks in many of the clauses in Appendix D.

You will note that the type of clause is given at the top of each page, such as "TERM OF PARTNERSHIP," or "OWNERSHIP INTERESTS." Within each type of clause, there may be several variation clauses that are numbered, such as "CLAUSE 1," or "CLAUSE 2." Usually you will need to choose one of these various clauses, although instructions may be given that more than one can be used.

There may also be other information to help you use that particular type of clause given after the heading "NOTE." These notes are not part of the clause, and are not to be used in your agreement. The actual clause to be used in the agreement will be the heading of the clause in bold print and the text of the paragraph that follows.

***Partnership Agreement Example***

On the following pages, you will find an example of a **PARTNERSHIP AGREEMENT** for a fictional group of partners, using the clauses from Appendix D. The left-hand page will give some information about the selection of the clauses, and the right-hand page will show one page of the **PARTNERSHIP AGREEMENT**.

This sample agreement is based on the following facts:

Three people, Alphonse Capone, Carry Nation, and Elliot Ness have decided to open a retail liquor store as partners. They have studied the forms in Appendix C and the various clauses in Appendix D, and decided to put together a **PARTNERSHIP AGREEMENT** using various clauses selected from Appendix D to fit their agreement.

In the next fourteen pages of this book, a copy of each page of their agreement is shown on the right-hand page and an explanation of what they did is on the left-hand page. The references to page numbers are to page numbers from Appendix D of this book.

❖ They have used the entire basic beginning clauses from page 149.

❖ Paragraph 4. They chose CLAUSE 1 from page 150.

❖ Paragraph 5. The partners have chosen not to use the general contributions clause on page 151. Instead, they have decided to combine several more specific contribution clauses under the general heading of CONTRIBUTIONS.

❖ Paragraph 5.A. They selected CLAUSE 2 from the CASH CONTRIBUTIONS section on page 152.

## PARTNERSHIP AGREEMENT

This Partnership Agreement is entered into this 23rd day of March, 2004, by and between the following partners: Alphonse Capone, Carry Nation, and Elliot Ness, who agree as follows:

**1. Name of Partnership.** The name of the partnership shall be: Valentine Enterprises.

The name under which the partnership shall conduct business shall be: Rumrunner's Warehouse.

**2. Principal Place of Business.** The partnership's principal place of business shall be:

413 Hatchet Place, Houston, Texas.

**3. Purpose of Partnership.** The purposes of the partnership are: operation of a retail liquor store.

In addition to the specific purposes set forth above, the purpose of the partnership is also to conduct any lawful business in which the partners, from time to time, may agree to become engaged.

**4. Term of Partnership.** The partnership shall become effective as of the date of this agreement, and shall continue until it is dissolved by all of the partners, or until any partner leaves for any reason including incapacity or death, or until otherwise dissolved by law.

**5. Contributions.**

**A. Cash Contributions.** Each partner shall make the following initial cash contribution to the partnership:

| Partner | Amount |
|---|---|
| Alphonse Capone | $40,000.00 |
| Carry Nation | $10,000.00 |
| Elliot Ness | $ 5,000.00 |

❖ Paragraph 5.B. They chose CLAUSE 1 from the NONCASH CONTRIBUTIONS section on page 153.

❖ Paragraph 5.C. This is CLAUSE 2 from page 156.

❖ As no loans are being made to the partnership by any partners, no clause was taken from page 158.

❖ Paragraph 6. Here the partners have combined CLAUSE 2 from page 159 with CLAUSES 1 and 2 from the DISTRIBUTION OF PROFITS section on page 160.

❖ Paragraph 7. Here they have combined CLAUSE 2 from the OWNER-SHIP INTERESTS section on page 162 and CLAUSE 3 from the VOTING RIGHTS section on page 163.

❖ The partners decided they did not need a *participation in partnership business* clause because they strongly believe that each of them will devote substantial time to participating in the business. (Time will tell whether this was a wise decision.)

❖ They have also decided that no partner salary clause is necessary, since there will be no salaries paid. (The absence of a statement on this subject could come back to haunt two of the partners if the third partner later sues them claiming that he or she was to have been paid a salary for extra work done.)

❖ Paragraph 8. This is CLAUSE 1 from the ACCOUNTING section on page 166.

❖ Paragraph 9. This is CLAUSE 2 from page 166.

**B. Contributions of Property.** The following partners shall contribute property to the partnership, of the type and value set forth below:

| Partner | Type of Property | Value |
|---|---|---|
| Carry Nation | Structure at 413 Hatchet Place | $20,000.00 |
| Elliot Ness | Liquor inventory | $25,000.00 |

**C. Additional Contributions.** No additional funds shall be required of any partner, unless the partners unanimously vote to contribute additional funds. In the event additional funds are needed, and a unanimous vote is not achieved, those partners desiring to continue the business and make the necessary contributions may do so, and each partner's percentage of ownership of the partnership and percentage of share in profits and losses shall be recalculated according to his or her percentage share of the total capital contribution of all partners.

**6. Profits and Losses.** Each partner shall share in the profits and losses of the partnership in proportion to each partner's percentage of ownership in the partnership as stated in paragraph 8 of this agreement. Any profits to which a partner shall be entitled, shall be determined and paid on a monthly basis. In determining the amount of profits available for distribution to partners, 30% of the total partnership profits shall be retained by the partnership for reinvestment in the partnership business, with the balance being distributed among the partners.

**7. Ownership Interests/Voting Rights/Decision Making.** Each partner's share of ownership in the partnership, with voting rights equal to each partner's percentage, shall be as follows:

| Partner | % of Ownership |
|---|---|
| Alphonse Capone | 40 |
| Carry Nation | 30 |
| Elliot Ness | 30 |

All partnership decisions shall be made by a majority vote of the partners. Each partner shall have a certain number of votes, which shall be equal to his or her percentage of ownership in the partnership as set forth in this agreement. In the event any proposal does not receive a majority vote, that proposal shall be deemed defeated.

**8. Partnership Accounting Records.** The partnership shall maintain proper and complete accounting records, in accordance with generally accepted accounting principals. Such records shall be kept at the partnership's principal place of business, and shall be available and open to all partners, or their representatives, for inspection at any time during regular business hours.

**9. Accounting to Partners.** An accounting of the partnership business, including profits and losses, shall be made to all partners at the close of each quarter. In addition, an accounting shall be made at any time upon the written request of any partner.

❖ Paragraph 10. This is a combination of CLAUSE 3 and CLAUSE 4 from pages 166 and 167.

❖ The partners decided that no one will have an expense account and that no expense account clause from page 168 is needed.

❖ Paragraphs 11 through 13. These are CLAUSES 1, 2, and 3 from the INSURANCE section on page 169.

❖ Paragraph 14. This is the partnership meeting clause from page 170.

❖ Paragraph 15.A. This is CLAUSE 1 from the TRANSFER OF PARTNER'S INTEREST section on page 171.

❖ Paragraph 15.B. This is CLAUSE 2 from page 171.

**10. Partnership Bank Accounts.** The partnership shall maintain at least one bank checking account, which shall bear the partnership name. Other bank accounts may be maintained as determined necessary by the partnership, however, all such accounts shall bear the partnership name. All partnership funds shall only be deposited in accounts bearing the partnership name.

All checks drawn on partnership checking accounts must be signed by at least 2 partners. All withdrawals of funds from other partnership accounts must be on the signature of at least 2 partners.

**11. Insurance of Business.** The partnership shall maintain policies of insurance to cover liability and business assets. Business asset insurance shall be sufficient to replace such assets. Liability insurance shall be in an amount determined by a majority vote of the partners.

**12. Life Insurance on Partners.** The partnership shall maintain a life insurance policy on each partner in the face value of $100,000. Said policy shall be an asset of the partnership.

**13. Disability Insurance on Partners.** The partnership shall maintain a disability insurance policy on each partner in the face value of $50,000. Said policy shall be an asset of the partnership.

**14. Partnership Meetings.** In order to discuss partnership business, the partners shall meet on the first Tuesday of each month, or at such other times as determined by a majority vote of the partners.

**15. Transfer of a Partner's Interest.**

**A. Option of Partnership to Purchase / Right of First Refusal.** In the event any partner leaves the partnership, for whatever reason, including voluntary withdrawal or retirement, expulsion, incapacity, or death, the remaining partner(s) shall have the option to purchase said partner's interest from said partner or his or her estate. In the event any partner receives, and is willing to accept, an offer from a person who is not a partner to purchase all of his or her interest in the partnership, he or she shall notify the other partners of the identity of the proposed buyer, the amount and terms of the offer, and of his or her willingness to accept the offer. The other partner(s) shall then have the option, within 30 days after notice is given, to purchase that partner's interest in the partnership on the same terms as those of the offer of the person who is not a partner.

**B. Option of Partnership to Sell or Dissolve Partnership.** In the event a partner leaves or receives an offer to purchase his or her interest as provided for in Paragraph 15.A. above, and the remaining partner(s) do not exercise the option to purchase, the remaining partners have the option to put the entire business up for sale, or to dissolve the partner-

❖ Paragraph 15.C. This is CLAUSE 3 from page 172.

❖ Paragraph 15.D. This is CLAUSE 7 from page 173.

❖ Paragraph 16. This is CLAUSE 2 from page 174.

❖ Paragraph 17. This is CLAUSE 1 from the ADMISSION OF NEW PARTNERS section on page 186.

**C. Valuation of Partnership.** In the event the remaining partners exercise their right to purchase another partner's interest as provided above, the value of the partnership shall be the net worth of the partnership as of the date of such purchase. Net worth shall be determined by the market value of the following assets: all of the partnership's real and personal property, liquid assets, accounts receivable, earned but unbilled fees, and money earned for work in progress; less the total amount of all debts owed by the partnership.

**D. Payment Upon Buy-Out.** In the event the remaining partners exercise their right to purchase another partner's interest as provided above, they shall pay the departing partner for his or her interest by way of a promissory note of the partnership, dated as of the date of purchase, which shall mature in not more than 3 years, and shall bear interest at the rate of 6% per annum. The first payment shall be made 30 days after the date of the promissory note.

**16. Expulsion of a Partner.** A partner shall be expelled from the partnership for any of the following reasons:

1. upon a unanimous vote of the other partners to expel a partner;
2. when the partner files a petition for relief under the Bankruptcy Code;
3. when the partner files for, or becomes subject to an order or decree of, insolvency under any state law;
4. when the partner files for, or becomes subject to, the appointment of a receiver or trustee over any of his or her assets which is not vacated within 60 days;
5. when the partner consents to, or becomes subject to, an attachment or execution of his or her assets that is not released within 60 days; or,
6. when the partner makes an assignment for the benefit of creditors.

Upon such expulsion, the expelled partner shall cease to be a partner and shall have no interest in the partnership or partnership property. Said partner's rights, powers and authorities, including the right to share in partnership profits, shall also cease. The expelled partner shall be considered a seller of his or her interest in the partnership as set forth in this agreement. In the event of any such expulsion, the partnership shall not be dissolved, but shall continue its business without interruption. The expulsion of any partner as provided above shall not be subject to mediation, arbitration, or review by any court.

**17. Admission of New Partners.** A new partner may join the partnership only with the unanimous written agreement of all of the partners, which shall include a revised agreement as to the ownership interests of the partners.

❖ Paragraph 18. This is CLAUSE 1 from the OWNERSHIP OF BUSINESS NAME section on page 176.

❖ Paragraph 19. This is CLAUSE 6 from page 178. None of the other asset ownership clauses were used because the partners felt that none of the other types of property would be used in their business. (If something changes later, they can always sign an amendment to the partnership agreement to cover the new situation.)

❖ Paragraph 20. This is CLAUSE 3 from page 179.

❖ Paragraph 21. This is CLAUSE 5 from page 180.

❖ Paragraph 22. This combines two of the mediation and arbitration clauses (from pages 181 and 183) under the heading "Dispute Resolution."

❖ Paragraph 22.A. This is CLAUSE 1 from page 181.

❖ Paragraph 22.B. This is CLAUSE 3 from page 183.

**18. Ownership of Business Name.** The business name of the partnership, Rumrunner's Warehouse, is owned by the partnership. No partner may use said name after leaving the partnership.

**19. Ownership of Trade Secrets.** All trade secrets used or developed by the partnership, including customer lists, supply sources, and computer programs, shall be owned and controlled by the partnership.

**20. Outside Business Activities.** Each partner may engage in other business activities, as long as such other business activities do not compete with, or interfere with, the business of the partnership; and do not conflict with the partner's obligations and time commitments to the partnership.

**21. Agreement Not to Compete.** It is agreed and understood that no partner, upon leaving the partnership, may engage in any business or activity that would compete with, or is similar to, the business of the partnership. This prohibition against competing with the partnership shall continue for a period of 5 years after leaving the partnership, and shall be limited to engaging in a similar business or activity within 150 miles of the partnership's place of business.

**22. Dispute Resolution.**

**A. Mediation of Disputes.** In the event of any dispute arising under this agreement, all partners agree that a resolution shall first be sought through mediation. As mediation is voluntary, all partners agree to cooperate with the mediator in attempting to resolve the dispute. It is agreed that J. Edgar Hoover shall serve as mediator, and that if such person is unable or unwilling to serve as mediator another mediator shall be chosen by mutual agreement of the partners to the dispute. Mediation shall be initiated by a written request for mediation, which shall be delivered to the other partners and the mediator. Mediation shall commence within 14 days after the request for mediation is delivered. Any agreement reached at through mediation shall be reduced to writing, shall be signed by all of the partners, and shall be binding upon all of the partners. Any costs of mediation shall be shared equally by all partners to the dispute.

**B. Arbitration.** In the event of any dispute arising under this agreement that could not be resolved through mediation, all partners agree that a resolution shall be sought through arbitration. Arbitration shall be initiated by a written request for arbitration, which shall state the nature of the dispute, the requesting partner's position, and shall name one person to serve as an arbitrator. Such request shall be delivered to the other partners. Arbitration shall proceed as follows:

❖ Paragraphs 23 through 28. These are the standard clauses from page 184.

1. Within 3 days after receiving the request for arbitration, the other partner shall have the right to deliver a response, which shall name a person to serve as the second arbitrator, and may state the responding partners' position. This response shall be delivered to the other party to the dispute.
2. Within 3 days after receiving a copy of the request and the response, the two designated arbitrators shall select a third arbitrator.
3. Within 7 days after selection of the third arbitrator, the arbitrators shall hold a hearing, at which time either party may present oral or written evidence. No partner may be represented by an attorney or any other third party.
4. The arbitrator shall issue a written decision within 7 days of the hearing date, which shall be delivered to both parties.
5. Any costs of arbitration shall be shared equally by all partners to the dispute.

**23. Continuity of Partnership.** In the event of a partner's voluntary withdrawal, expulsion, death, or incapacity, the partnership shall not terminate or dissolve, but shall continue its business without any break in continuity.

**24. Governing Law.** This agreement shall be governed by the laws of Texas.

**25. Severability.** If any part of this agreement is adjudged invalid, illegal, or unenforceable, the remaining parts shall not be affected and shall remain in full force and effect.

**26. Binding Agreement / No Other Beneficiary.** This agreement shall be binding upon the parties, and upon their heirs, executors, personal representatives, administrators, and assigns. No person shall have a right or cause of action arising or resulting from this agreement except those who are parties to it and their successors in interest.

**27. Entire Agreement.** This instrument, including any attached exhibits, constitutes the entire agreement of the parties. No representations or promises have been made except those that are set out in this agreement. This agreement may not be modified except in writing signed by all the parties.

❖    For signatures, the partners decided to have a separate date line above each partner's signature line.

**28. Paragraph Headings.** The headings of the paragraphs contained in this agreement are for convenience only, and are not to be considered a part of this agreement or used in determining its content or context.

Dated:_____        Dated:_____

_____     _____
Alphonse Capone                Elliot Ness

Dated:_____

_____
Carry Nation

# 6 CHANGING PARTNERS

Some partnerships find it necessary to drop or add partners. Traditionally, any change of partners was actually the termination of the old partnership and the formation of a new partnership. Today, partners are added and dropped almost the same as shareholders in a corporation. This may occur in various ways.

- ✪ The partnership *buys out* the departing partner's interest (no new partner is admitted to the partnership).

- ✪ The new partner buys the departing partner's interest (one partner leaves and another is admitted).

- ✪ A new partner buys into the partnership (no partner leaves).

There can also be the situation where the partnership buys out the departing partner's interest and admits a new partner (with the same or different percentage interest than the departing partner), but this is really just a combination of the first and third on the list above. Each of these situations will be handled differently.

The two main concerns are the financial arrangement between the parties and the liability of the departing or incoming partner for the partnership debts and obligations. For an example, take a look at what the *Uniform Partnership Act* says about these matters.

# Uniform Partnership Act

First of all, the *Uniform Partnership Act* (UPA) states in Section 29 that a *dissolution* of the partnership occurs whenever a partner ceases to be associated with the carrying on of the partnership business. This does not discontinue the business, but does require there to be a settlement of financial affairs with the departing partner. Section 40 sets forth how the financial affairs will be settled, unless there is an agreement to the contrary. Where there is an agreement, the agreement will control. With respect to creditors of the partnership, Section 36 provides that the departing partner remains personally liable for debts and obligations to third parties. While the remaining partners can agree to indemnify the outgoing partner, he or she will remain liable as to the third party creditors unless released from liability.

The **PARTNERSHIP AGREEMENT** should be written so it covers the buy-out of a departing partner's interest by the partnership. See paragraph 8 of form 1, paragraphs 20 and 21 of form 2, and the "Transfer of Partner's Interest" and "Expulsion of a Partner" clauses on pages 171 through 175 in Appendix D. If this situation is not covered sufficiently in your **PARTNERSHIP AGREEMENT**, or even if it is covered but you want to clearly set forth your agreement in writing, you can use the **PARTNERSHIP BUY-OUT AGREEMENT** in Appendix C. (see form 4, p.137.) This form will be discussed later in this chapter.

The UPA does not have much to say about the financial arrangement between existing partners and a new partner. Section 27 provides that the purchase of a partner's interest does not allow the purchaser to participate in the business or obtain any information. All the purchaser is entitled to is the seller's share of the profits. The paragraphs in this book, which allow the partners the right of first refusal to purchase, should eliminate most problems with unwanted partners coming in through a sale of a partner's interest.

The incoming partner's relationship to the original partners should be covered by an **AMENDMENT TO PARTNERSHIP AGREEMENT**. (see form 5, p.141.) At a minimum, this amendment should state the contribution of the new partner and the share of profits and losses and percentage of ownership interests of all partners.

It should also contain a provision that the new partner agrees to be bound by all of the terms of the original partnership agreement. (Form 5 will be discussed in more detail later in this chapter.)

Regarding the liability of the new partner, Section 17 of the Uniform Partnership Act provides that he or she will be liable for the existing debts of the partnership, but only to the extent of his or her share of the partnership property. This means that the new partner will not be subject to losing his or her individual, personal property to satisfy partnership debts incurred before he or she became a partner. Of course, this can be changed by a written agreement signed by the new partner.

# Departing Partner Sells to Partnership

There may come a time when a partner will sell his or her partnership interest to the partnership itself. This may occur if a partner and the partnership agree to separate, if a partner gets an offer to purchase and the partnership exercises its right to purchase, or if a partner is expelled according to the terms of the partnership agreement.

If the **PARTNERSHIP AGREEMENT** is drafted to cover this situation, a new agreement may not be necessary. However, it may still be a good idea to prepare a **PARTNERSHIP BUY-OUT AGREEMENT** (form 4, p.137), just to be sure that everyone is in agreement. You will also need a buy-out agreement if you wish to vary the buy-out terms from those in your **PARTNERSHIP AGREEMENT**.

To complete the **PARTNERSHIP BUY-OUT AGREEMENT** (form 4) you need to:

◈ Fill in the appropriate date and names in the first, unnumbered, paragraph.

◈ In paragraph 1, fill in the date of the original partnership agreement, the name of the partnership, and the principal place of business. This information will be found in your original **PARTNERSHIP AGREEMENT**.

◈ In paragraph 4(a), fill in the amount that will be paid to the seller for his or her interest in the partnership. Then check one of the boxes for how payment will be made and fill in any blanks with the appropriate information.

◈ Paragraph 5 is to amend the partnership agreement to reflect the new ownership, profits, and losses ratios of the remaining partners. This paragraph is optional, and need not be used if there is a paragraph in the original **PARTNERSHIP AGREEMENT** providing for such an adjustment, or if there is going to be a separate amendment agreement prepared.

◈ In paragraph 6, type in the date after which the departing partner may engage in activities that may compete with the partnership. Review your **PARTNERSHIP AGREEMENT** to see what it says on the subject of competition, and look at the "Other Business Activity and Noncompetition" clauses in Appendix D.

◈ If the partnership provided insurance for the partners, indicate in paragraph 7 the type of coverage (e.g., life, disability, auto) and the date coverage will terminate for the outgoing partner. If life insurance is to be terminated, delete the first sentence of this paragraph.

◈ Fill in the name of your state in paragraph 11.

◈ Have all of the partners, including the outgoing partner, sign after paragraph 13.

An example of a **PARTNERSHIP BUY-OUT AGREEMENT** is found on the following two pages.

## PARTNERSHIP BUY-OUT AGREEMENT

This Partnership Buy-Out Agreement is entered into this _____**14th**_____ day of _____**February**_____, _____**2005**_____, by and between _____**Alphonse Capone**_____, (hereinafter referred to as "Seller"), and_____**Carry Nation and Elliot Ness**_____, (hereinafter referred to as "Buyers"), who agree as follows:

**1. Partnership.** The above named parties hereto have been and are now partners doing business pursuant to a Partnership Agreement dated ___**March 23, 2004**___, under the name of _____**Valentine Enterprises**_____, with its principal place of business in _____**Houston, Texas**_____.

**2. Agreement to Purchase and Sell.** The Buyers hereby agree to purchase, and the Seller hereby agrees to sell, all of the Seller's interest in the partnership according to the terms of this Partnership Buy-Out Agreement.

**3. Valuation.** The parties agree that each partnership asset has a present fair market value equal to its book value to the partnership, as reflected in the partnership financial records, and that any consideration in this agreement that is in excess of book value is attributable to goodwill not shown in the partnership financial records.

**4. Purchase.** The Buyers hereby purchase, and the Seller hereby sells, all of the Seller's interest in the partnership and partnership property, in consideration of:

    a.    The payment to the Seller of $_____**40,000.00**_____, to be paid:

        ☒    In full in cash, check, or money order, to be paid within 30 days after the date of this agreement.

        ❏    A negotiable promissory note in the form of Exhibit A attached hereto.

        ❏    The sum of $_____ to be paid in cash within 30 days after the date of this agreement, and a negotiable promissory note for the balance in the form of Exhibit A attached hereto.

    b.    The agreement of the Buyer's and the partnership to hold the Seller free and harmless from all partnership debts and liabilities.

**5. Amendment of Partnership Agreement.** The Partnership Agreement is hereby amended to provide that from and after the date of this agreement, only the Buyers shall exercise management and control over partnership decisions, and that from and after that date, the ownership, profits and losses of the partnership will be shared by the Buyers as follows:

| Partner | % Ownership | % Profits | % Losses |
|---|---|---|---|
| Carry Nation | 50% | 50% | 50% |
| Elliot Ness | 50% | 50% | 50% |
| | | | |

**6. Competition Permitted.** From and after _____ February 14 _____, _2005_, the Seller shall be free to conduct consulting activities apart from the partnership, even to the extent of competing with the partnership.

**7. Insurance.** The Seller shall be entitled to assume the life insurance policy on his or her life presently carried by the partnership, but shall be required to maintain all future premium payments. The Seller shall continue to receive insurance coverage under the partnership's policies as follows:

| Type of Insurance | Coverage Termination Date |
|---|---|
| Medical | March 31, 2005 |
| Disability | March 1, 2005 |

**8. Partnership Name.** The Seller shall not use the partnership's name or any name confusingly similar thereto in any new business activity conducted by him or her. The Seller may refer to the partnership name solely for purposes of indicating transition from the partnership to his or her new business, or to the extent necessary to identify prior projects that the Seller has completed.

**9. Disclosure.** Except as appears in the books of the partnership, each of the partners represents that he or she has not heretofore contracted any liability that can or may charge the partnership or any other partner, nor has he or she received or discharged any of the credits, monies, or effects of the partnership.

**10. Continuity of Partnership.** After the Seller's departure from the partnership, the partnership shall not terminate or dissolve, but shall continue its business without any break in continuity.

**11. Governing Law.** This agreement shall be governed by the laws of ___ Texas ___.

**12. Binding Agreement / No Other Beneficiary.** This agreement shall be binding upon the parties, and upon their heirs, executors, personal representatives, administrators, and assigns. No person shall have a right or cause of action arising or resulting from this agreement except those who are parties to it and their successors in interest.

**13. Entire Agreement.** This instrument, including any attached exhibits, constitutes the entire agreement of the parties with respect to this buy-out. No representations or promises have been made except those that are set out in this agreement. This agreement may not be modified except in writing signed by all the parties.

| | |
|---|---|
| *Alphonse Capone* | *Carry Nation* |
| Alphonse Capone | Carry Nation |
| *Elliot Ness* | |
| Elliot Ness | |

# New Partner Purchases from Existing Partner

One partner selling his or her interest to a new party may often only be done with the agreement of the other partners. Otherwise the other partners could invoke their *right of first refusal,* providing there was such a provision in the **PARTNERSHIP AGREEMENT**. If there was not such a provision or the partners did not want the new person but could not afford to purchase the share, there will simply be an agreement between the buyer and seller, outlining the terms of the sale. In such cases, the new partner is not entitled to full participation in the business. The original remaining partners will generally need only pay the purchaser his or her appropriate share of the profits. (Some states have modified the UPA to give the purchaser certain other limited rights, such as the right to inspect partnership books.)

When there is a purchase of one partner's interest, there will probably be two agreements: one between the buyer and seller and an amendment to the original partnership agreement. The agreement between the buyer and seller will simply state the terms of the sale, such as a description of the seller's interest in the partnership, the purchase price, and how the purchase price is to be paid.

In Appendix C there is an **AMENDMENT TO PARTNERSHIP AGREEMENT**. (see form 5, p.141.) It can be used for the agreement between the new partner and the remaining original partners. The sample **AMENDMENT TO PARTNERSHIP AGREEMENT** that follows is for the situation where a new partner is purchasing the share of an existing partner.

❖ First, unnumbered, paragraph. This is the date the **AMENDMENT TO PARTNERSHIP AGREEMENT** is signed. The names of all partners, old and new, should be included.

❖ Paragraph 1. These spaces are for the name of the partnership, and the date of the original partnership agreement.

❖ Paragraph 1.a. This provision shows the change of the partnership interest from the seller to the buyer.

❖ Paragraph 1.b. This section spells out the percentage of ownership between the new partner and the remaining original partners. In this example, the purchaser simply takes the same ownership interest as the seller. However, this could be different if the new partner were also going to contribute additional money or property to the partnership.

❖ All partners, new and old, should sign.

## AMENDMENT TO PARTNERSHIP AGREEMENT

This Amendment to Partnership Agreement is entered into on ____June 21____, ____2004____, by and between _____
__Alphonse Capone, Carry Nation, Elliot Ness, and Jim Brady__
_____, who agree as follows:

1.  The Partnership Agreement for _____Valentine Enterprises_____, dated _____March 23, 2004_____, is hereby amended to read as follows:

a.  Alphonse Capone shall be deleted as a partner, and Jim Brady shall be admitted as a partner.

b.  Paragraph 8 shall be amended to read as follows:

**8.  Ownership Interests/Voting Rights/Decision Making.** Each partner's share of ownership in the partnership, with voting rights equal to each partner's percentage, shall be as follows:

| Partner | % of Ownership |
|---|---|
| Carry Nation | 30% |
| Elliot Ness | 30% |
| Jim Brady | 40% |

All partnership decisions shall be made by a majority vote of the partners. Each partner shall have a certain number of votes, which shall be equal to his or her percentage of ownership in the partnership as set forth in this agreement. In the event any proposal does not receive a majority vote, that proposal shall be deemed defeated.

2.  In all other respects not referred to herein, said Partnership Agreement is ratified and confirmed, and shall remain in full force and effect.


*Alphonse Capone*                    *Elliot Ness*
Alphonse Capone                      Elliot Ness


*Carry Nation*                       *Jim Brady*
Carry Nation                         Jim Brady

# New Partner Buys into Existing Partnership

Having a new partner come into the partnership may be done to raise more money or to acquire the skills or assets of the new partner. This will require the **AMENDMENT TO PARTNERSHIP AGREEMENT** (form 5, p.141) to reflect the new partner's contribution and the new portion of each partner's interest in profits, losses, and ownership.

The **AMENDMENT TO PARTNERSHIP AGREEMENT** on page 61 is for the situation where a new, additional partner is being admitted. The new partner is contributing money and all of the original partners will stay in the partnership. The following comments will help you understand this agreement.

❖ First, unnumbered, paragraph. This is the date the **AMENDMENT TO PARTNERSHIP AGREEMENT** is signed. All partners' names should be listed, including the new partner.

❖ Paragraph 1. These spaces are for the name of the partnership and the date of the original partnership agreement.

❖ Paragraph 1.a. This space is for the name of the new partner, and the amount of money or other property he or she will contribute. If property is contributed, you will need to describe the property and list its value.

❖ Paragraph 1.b. This provision is for re-computing each partner's ownership interest after the new partner comes into the partnership. In this example, the new partner is contributing $25,000. This will add to the cash and property contributions of the original partners, and will change each partner's share of the total contributions. The original partners contributed a total of $100,000 in cash and property. Jim Brady's cash contribution brings this total up to $125,000. Now Capone's share is 32% ($40,000 Capone contributed divided by $125,000 total contributions). Nation and Ness each have a 24% interest ($30,000 contribution each divided by $125,000 total contributions). Brady has a 20% share ($25,000 Brady contribution divided by $125,000 total contributions).

❖ All partners, new and old, need to sign.

# AMENDMENT TO PARTNERSHIP AGREEMENT

This Amendment to Partnership Agreement is entered into on _____May 6_____, __2004__, by and between _____ _Alphonse Capone, Carry Nation, Elliot Ness, and Jim Brady_ _____,
who agree as follows:

1.     The Partnership Agreement for _____Valentine Enterprises_____,
dated _____March 23, 2004_____, is hereby amended to read as follows:

a.     Paragraph 5 is amended to add subparagraph C as follows:

**C. Contribution of New Partner.** Partner Jim Brady shall make the following cash contribution to the partnership as an incoming partner: $25,000.00.

b.     Paragraph 8 is amended to read as follows:

**8. Ownership Interests / Voting Rights / Decision Making.** Each partner's share of ownership in the partnership, with voting rights equal to each partner's percentage, shall be as follows:

| Partner | % of Ownership |
|---|---|
| Alphonse Capone | 32% |
| Carry Nation | 24% |
| Elliot Ness | 24% |
| Jim Brady | 20% |

All partnership decisions shall be made by a majority vote of the partners. Each partner shall have a certain number of votes, which shall be equal to his or her percentage of ownership in the partnership as set forth in this agreement. In the event any proposal does not receive a majority vote, that proposal shall be deemed defeated.

2.     In all other respects not referred to herein, said Partnership Agreement is ratified and confirmed, and shall remain in full force and effect.

*Alphonse Capone*
Alphonse Capone

*Carry Nation*
Carry Nation

*Elliot Ness*
Elliot Ness

*Jim Brady*
Jim Brady

Form 5, the **AMENDMENT TO PARTNERSHIP AGREEMENT**, can be used for the admission of a new partner. This should at least include new paragraphs about any of the following provisions that were in the original partnership agreement:

✪   the partners' contributions;

✪   share of profits and losses;

✪   ownership interests;

✪   voting rights;

✪   participation in partnership business; and,

✪   any other matters you need to cover for your particular situation.

# 7 | DISSOLVING A PARTNERSHIP

At some time, you and your partners may decide to end your partnership. This is called *dissolving* the partnership. It may occur when you are ready for retirement, the business is no longer profitable, or for a number of other reasons. In general, Sections 29 through 40 of the UPA discuss this process. Sections 31 and 32 state when dissolution may occur. Whatever the reason, there are certain things that must be done.

Dissolving a partnership is basically a four-step process.

1. Stop doing business.

2. Sell the partnership assets.

3. Pay off all creditors.

4. Divide the balance between the partners.

Of course, before you begin these steps, you and your partners must first meet and discuss dissolution. To make sure you are all in agreement and that the dissolution goes as smoothly as possible, you may want to sign a **PARTNERSHIP**

**TERMINATION AGREEMENT**. (see form 3, p.133.) You can either use the form provided as it is, or modify it as needed to fit your agreement.

To complete form 3 you need to:

◈ Fill in the date of the termination agreement and the names of the partners in the appropriate spaces in the first, unnumbered, paragraph.

◈ In paragraph 1, type in the date of your original partnership agreement in the first space, the name of the partnership in the second space, and the location of the partnership in the third space. This is to clearly identify the partnership, which probably will not be a problem unless you and your partners have more than one partnership.

◈ In paragraph 4, fill in a date for all partners to stop conducting any new business. This can be the date of the termination agreement, or any date thereafter.

◈ In paragraph 5.A., type in a date for an accounting to be performed. This date will serve as the basis for determining the value of the business.

◈ The spaces in paragraph 5.C., are for you to list any special assets that are to be distributed to particular partners.

***Example:*** If one partner contributed a computer to the partnership, you may want the computer returned to that person, instead of selling it with the other assets. Or one partner who is continuing in another business might want a particular asset. If no assets are to be distributed you may either leave this paragraph out of your termination agreement, or type in *None* under the heading "Asset."

If you do list any assets, fill in a description of the asset, its book value, and the name of the partner who will receive the asset. The book value will then be used as part of that partner's share of the distribution.

◈ In paragraph 7, type in the period of time (such as *6 months*, or *1 year*, etc.) during which no partner may use the partnership name in a new business venture. This paragraph is not absolutely necessary, but it is a good idea so that creditors do not mistakenly assume the partnership is still in business.

◈    In paragraph 8, type in the name of your state.

◈    Finally, spaces are provided after paragraph 10 for all partners to sign.

The next step is to begin carrying out the terms of your agreement. This is referred to as *winding up* the partnership business. Section 37 of the UPA refers to winding up. This involves closing the doors to your customers, and notifying your creditors that you are going out of business. You will then need to pay all of the partnership's outstanding debts, selling assets if necessary to raise the needed cash. Once this is done the balance will be distributed among the partners. Either all assets can be sold and cash distributed, or a combination of assets and cash can be distributed. Such distribution should be according to each partner's right to receive profits.

If there are not enough assets to enable the partnership to pay off creditors, each partner may need to contribute personal funds to accomplish this. Otherwise all partners are subject to suit by the unpaid creditors.

A sample completed **PARTNERSHIP TERMINATION AGREEMENT** is found on the next two pages.

## PARTNERSHIP TERMINATION AGREEMENT

This Partnership Termination Agreement is entered into this \_\_\_\_**18th**\_\_\_\_ day of _____**June**_____, \_\_**2005**\_\_, by and between the following partners: **Alphonse Capone, Carry Nation, Elliot Ness, and Jim Brady**_____,
who agree as follows:

**1. Partnership.** The above named parties have been and are now partners doing business pursuant to a Partnership Agreement dated _____**March 24, 2004**_____, under the name of _____**Valentine Enterprises**_____, with its principal place of business in _____**Houston, Texas**_____.

**2. Agreement to Dissolve Partnership.** The partners hereby agree to dissolve their partnership and liquidate its affairs, according to the provisions of this agreement.

**3. Valuation of Partnership Assets.** The partners agree that each partnership asset has a present fair market value equal to its book value to the partnership as reflected on the partnership financial records, unless any such asset is sold in which event that asset shall be deemed to have a value equal to its sale price.

**4. Termination of Partnership Business.** After \_\_**October 24**\_\_\_\_\_, \_**2005**\_, no partner shall do any further business nor incur any further obligations on behalf of the partnership. except for the purposes of carrying out the liquidation of the partnership and the winding-up of partnership affairs.

**5. Liquidation.** Liquidation of the partnership shall proceed as follows:

**A. Accounting.** The partnership accountant shall perform an accounting of all assets and liabilities of the partnership, and of the respective equities of the creditors and the partners in the assets, as of the date such accounting is performed. Such accounting shall be performed no later than \_\_**October 31**\_\_\_\_, \_**2005**\_\_.

**B. Settling Accounts.** Upon completion of the accounting, the partners shall pay all of the liabilities of the partnership, including those owing to the partners other than for capital contributions. Payment of liabilities owing to the partners shall include payment of profits for the current accounting period computed on the basis of actual cash receipts through the date of the accounting. Any funds received after the date of the accounting shall be distributed among the partners according to each partner's percentage of ownership in the partnership.

**C. Distribution of Partnership Assets.** Any partnership assets remaining after payment of all partnership liabilities shall be sold, with the proceeds being divided among the partners according to each partner's percentage of ownership in the partnership. Each partner shall have the right to purchase any partnership asset at book value, before any sale to a non-partner. The following assets shall be transferred to individual partners as their individual property as indicated below:

| Asset | Book Value | Partner Becoming Owner |
|---|---|---|
| Structure at 413 Hatchet Pl. | $19,000 | Carry Nation |
| Liquor inventory | $10,000 | Elliot Ness |
| | | |
| | | |

**6. Disclosure.** Except as appears in the books of the partnership, each of the partners represents that he or she has not heretofore contracted any liability that can or may charge the partnership or the other partner, nor has he or she received or discharged any of the credits, monies or effects of the partnership.

**7. Partnership Name.** No partner shall use the partnership's name or any name confusingly similar thereto in any new business activity for a period of _____18 months_____. Until that time any partner shall be entitled to refer to the partnership name solely for purposes of a transition from the partnership to his or her new business, or to the extent necessary to explain such partner's employment and work history.

**8. Governing Law.** This agreement shall be governed by the laws of ___Texas___.

**9. Binding Agreement / No Other Beneficiary.** This agreement shall be binding upon the parties, and upon their heirs, executors, personal representatives, administrators, and assigns. No person shall have a right or cause of action arising or resulting from this agreement except those who are parties to it and their successors in interest.

**10. Entire Agreement.** This instrument, including any attached exhibits, constitutes the entire agreement of the parties with respect to the termination of the partnership. No representations or promises have been made except those that are set out in this agreement. This agreement may not be modified except in writing signed by all the parties.

*Alphonse Capone*
Alphonse Capone

*Elliot Ness*
Elliot Ness

*Carry Nation*
Carry Nation

*Jim Brady*
Jim Brady

# 8 LOOKING FORWARD

As you conduct your business, keep in mind that forming your partnership is not necessarily an end in itself. Like any business entity, a partnership is an ever-changing operation. Partners may come; partners may leave; and, the business climate changes. Along with considering how to best change with the times to keep your business competitive and profitable, you may need to consider whether your partnership agreement needs to change, or even whether the form of your business should change.

As your partnership becomes larger or more profitable, you may want to consider changing to a corporation or limited liability company. This will largely be determined by tax ramifications and your potential for personal liability for partnership activities.

For now, congratulations on your new partnership, and good luck on becoming very profitable!

# GLOSSARY

**NOTE:** *This glossary provides general definitions. Any of these terms may be specifically defined by the laws of your state. If any term is specifically defined by the laws of your state, that definition will be used by a court or governmental agency in interpreting any partnership agreement you may create. In addition to the following definitions, see the definitions contained in the UPA, the RUPA, and the particular partenership law of your state.*

## A

**acknowledgment.** A statement, written or oral, made before a person authorized by law to administer oaths (such as a notary public).

**adult.** In most states, a person eighteen years of age or older.

**affiant.** The legal term for the person who signs an affidavit.

**affidavit.** A person's written statement of facts, signed under oath before a person authorized to administer oaths (such as a notary public or court clerk).

**agent.** A person who is given authority to act on behalf of another person or other legal entity.

**arbitration.** A type of dispute resolution, whereby one or more persons (called *arbitrators*) determine the outcome of the dispute, similar to the manner in which a judge makes a decision in a lawsuit. Arbitration can either be binding (meaning that the decision of the arbitrators is final) or nonbinding (meaning that either party can file a lawsuit to have the matter heard in a court). The idea is that arbitration is quicker and less expensive than a lawsuit in court, however, this is not always the case in practice.

**articles of incorporation.** A legal document filed with a state government to set up a corporation.

**articles of organization.** A legal document filed with a state government to set up a limited liability company.

**assumed name.** A name under which a person, partnership, corporation, or other business entity conducts business.

# B

**blue sky laws.** A common name for laws regulating investments and securities.

**buy-out.** When someone, or the partnership itself, purchases the partnership interest of one of the partners.

# C

**C corporation.** A corporation that pays taxes on its profits.

**certificate of limited partnership.** A legal document filed with the state government to register a limited partnership.

**common law.** Legal principals that are determined in court cases, rather than statutes enacted by a legislature.

**corporation.** An artificial person that is set up to conduct business owned by shareholders and run by officers and directors.

**creditor.** A person or institution to whom money is owed.

# D

**d/b/a.** Abbreviation for doing business as.

**debtor.** A person or institution who owes money.

**dissolution.** The termination of a partnership.

**distribution.** A transfer of money or other property from a partnership to a partner in the partner's capacity as a partner or to the partner's transferee.

# E

**execute.** To sign a legal document, in the legally required manner (e.g., before witnesses or a notary public), thereby making it effective.

# F

**fictitious name.** *See assumed name.*

**fiduciary.** A person having a duty, created by his or her own undertaking, to act primarily for the benefit of another; requiring scrupulous good faith.

# G

**general partner.** A partner in a limited partnership who has authority to engage in operating the business.

**good will.** In accounting, the monetary value placed on the good reputation of a business. It is considered an asset of the business. Typically, an organization that has been in business for a number of years and enjoys a good reputation among its customers has more good will value than a new company.

# I

**instrument.** A legal term for a document.

**intellectual property.** Legal rights to the products of the mind, such as writings, musical compositions, formulas, and designs.

# J

**joint tenancy.** A way for two or more people to own property, so that when one owner dies, his or her interest in the property passes automatically to the remaining owner or owners.

# L

**lessee.** One who rents property from another.

**lessor.** One who rents property to another.

**liability.** The legal responsibility to pay for debts, damages, or injuries.

**limited liability company.** An artificial person that is set up to conduct business owned and run by members, who have no personal liability business obligations.

**limited partner.** A partner in a limited partnership who is in the position of an investor, and has no authority to engage in operating the business.

# M

**mediation.** A form of dispute resolution in which a person called a *mediator* attempts to help the parties reach a mutually agreeable settlement of the dispute. Mediation is different from arbitration in that the mediator does not make a decision, as does an arbitrator.

# N

**notary public.** A person who is legally authorized by the state to acknowledge signatures on legal documents.

# P

**partnership.** An association of two or more persons to carry on as co-owners a business for profit.

**partnership agreement.** An agreement, written or oral, among the partners concerning the partnership, including amendments to the partnership agreement.

**partnership at will.** A partnership in which the partners have not agreed to remain partners until the expiration of a definite term or the completion of a particular undertaking.

**partnership interest.** All of a partner's interests in the partnership, including the partner's transferable interest and all management and other rights.

**personal property.** All property other than land and things permanently attached to the land (such as buildings).

# R

**real property.** Land and the structures attached to it.

**recording.** The process of filing a deed, mortgage, or other legal document affecting title to land, with the court clerk's office.

**registration statement.** A legal document that is filed with a state government to register a partnership. This is optional in most states.

**Revised Uniform Partnership Act (RUPA).** A standardized partnership law, created as an improvement on the UPA, which has been adopted by many states.

**right of first refusal.** In partnership law, the right of the partnership to purchase the interest of a partner before that partner may sell his or her interest to a third party.

# S

**S corporation.** A corporation that is taxed as a partnership under IRS rules.

**securities.** Interests in a business, such as stocks or bonds.

**sole proprietorship.** A business owned by an individual.

# T

**tenancy by the entirety.** This is essentially the same as joint tenancy, but it can only occur between a husband and wife. Upon the death of one spouse, the property automatically passes to the surviving spouse. In states that do not have a tenancy by the entirety, spouses typically hold property as joint tenants with rights of survivorship.

**tenancy in common.** A way for two or more people to own property, whereby if one of the owners dies, his or her interest in the property passes to his or her heirs (not to the other co-owners).

**trade name.** A name used to identify the manufacturer of a product or group of products.

**trademark.** A distinguishing mark used to identify the manufacturer of a product or group of products.

# U

**Uniform Partnership Act (UPA).** A standardized partnership law that has been adopted by many states.

# W

**winding up.** The acts connected with closing business operations upon the dissolution of a partnership.

# APPENDIX A:
# STATE PARTNERSHIP LAWS

This appendix contains a state-by-state reference guide to the partnership laws of each state and the District of Columbia. Under each state's listing, you will find a reference to the partnership law of that state, along with some information to help you locate the proper set of books or website. This will be the reference to the state's UPA or RUPA (except for Louisiana, which has its own partnership act that is not based on the UPA or RUPA).

**Example:** The RUPA as adopted by Alabama is found in the Code of Alabama, at Title 10, Chapter 8A, Section 10-8A-101. This is abbreviated "C.A. §10-8A-101." "C.A." stands for Code of Alabama.

**NOTE:** *"§" is a symbol for the word section. "§§" is a symbol for the word sections.*

If the state has designated an official short title for its partnership law, that designation will appear in quotation marks.

**Example:** Alabama has designated its law as the "Alabama Uniform Partnership Act."

**NOTE:** *"§" is a symbol for the word section. "§§" is a symbol for the word sections.*

If you see the word "Titled" before the designation, it means that the state has not officially designated this as the short title, but only uses it as a heading for the law.

> **Example:** The partnership law in Arizona is titled "Revised Uniform Partnership Act," but the law itself does not say "This act shall be known as the Revised Uniform Partnership Act."

Some states have listings for both the UPA and the RUPA. In these states, the UPA is being repealed at some future date, and replaced with the RUPA. Typically, there is an overlap period, so that partnerships that were formed under the UPA can still operate under that act during a transition period.

If you have any difficulty finding the partnership laws for your state, ask the law librarian for assistance.

## STATE LAW REFERENCE GUIDE

You may find all states' statutes on the Internet, although they can vary dramatically in user-friendliness. Some of these sites are maintained by the state government. Others are maintained by private companies or law firms. For some states, the laws are also available by paying for a subscription service. A single site, **www.findlaw.com**, provides access to all of the state websites. The sites listed below for individual states are the same sites that Findlaw will take you to, but they are provided here because you may wish to skip a few of the steps in getting to them through Findlaw. These sites may change at any time, so if you have any problems accessing a site listed below, try the Findlaw site. Additional help in navigating a particular state's website may also be included below.

*ALL STATES:*     **www.findlaw.com** Once you get to the Findlaw site, click on "US State Resources," then click on the name of the state you want; click on "Primary Materials-Cases, Codes and Regulations," then click on the state code or statutes.

*ALABAMA*     **RUPA:** Code of Alabama 1975, Title 10, Chapter 8A, Section 10-8A-101 (C.A. §10-8A-101). "Alabama Uniform Partnership Act."

**Website:** www.legislature.state.al.us/ALISHome.html

*ALASKA*     **UPA:** Alaska Statutes, Title 32, Section 32.06.201 (A.S. §32.06.201).

**Website:** www.legis.state.ak.us/folhome.htm

**NOTE:** *"§" is a symbol for the word section. "§§" is a symbol for the word sections.*

*ARIZONA*  **RUPA:** Arizona Revised Statutes, Title 29, Section 29-1001 (A.R.S. §29-1001). Titled "Revised Uniform Partnership Act."

**Website:** www.azleg.state.az.us/ArizonaRevisedStatutes.asp

*ARKANSAS*  **UPA:** Arkansas Code of 1987 Annotated, Title 4, Chapter 42, Section 4-42-101 (A.C.A. §4-42-101). Titled "Uniform Partnership Act." This act will be repealed effective 1/1/05. Until then, it applies to partnerships formed before 1/1/00 and those formed afterward, if continuing the business of a partnership dissolved pursuant to section 33. A partnership formed before 1/1/00 may elect to be governed by the new Uniform Partnership Act (1996).

**RUPA:** A.C.A. §4-46-101. Titled "Uniform Partnership Act" (1996). Before 1/1/05, this act governs partnerships formed after 1/1/00, unless the partnership is continuing the business of a partnership dissolved under the UPA; and governs partnerships formed before 1/1/00 if they so elect. It will govern all partnerships beginning 1/1/05.

**Website:** www.arkleg.state.ar.us/2003/data/ACSA.asp

*CALIFORNIA*  **RUPA:** West's Annotated California Codes, Corporation Code, Section 16100 (A.C.C., Corp. Code §16100). "Uniform Partnership Act of 1994."

**Website:** www.leginfo.ca.gov/calaw.html

*COLORADO*  **RUPA:** West's Colorado Revised Statutes Annotated, Title 7, Article 64, Section 7-64-101 (C.R.S.A. §7-64-101). "Colorado Uniform Partnership Act (1997)."

**Website:** 198.187.128.12/colorado/lpext.dll?f=templates&fn=fs-main.htm&2.0

*CONNECTICUT*  **RUPA:** Connecticut General Statutes Annotated, Title 34, Section 34-300 (C.G.S.A. §34-300). "Uniform Partnership Act (1994)."

**Website:** www.cga.state.ct.us/asp/menu/Statutes.asp

*DELAWARE*  **RUPA:** Delaware Code Annotated, Title 6, Article 15, Section 15-101 (D.C.A. 6 §15-101). "Delaware Revised Uniform Partnership Act."

**Website:** www.delcode.state.de.us

**NOTE:** *"§" is a symbol for the word section. "§§" is a symbol for the word sections.*

**DISTRICT OF COLUMBIA**

**UPA:** District of Columbia Code, Title 33, Section 33-101-01 (D.C.C. §33-101-01).

**Website:** http://dccode.westgroup.com

**NOTE:** *Click on "DIVISION V. LOCAL BUSINESS AFFAIRS."*

**FLORIDA**

**RUPA:** Florida Statutes, Chapter 620, Sections 620.81001 to 620.8908 (F.S. §620-81001). "Revised Uniform Partnership Act of 1995."

**Website:** www.flsenate.gov/statutes

**GEORGIA**

**UPA:** Official Code of Georgia Annotated, Title 14, Chapter 8, Section 14-8-1 (C.G.A. §14-8-1). "Uniform Partnership Act." [This is not the Georgia Code, which is a separate set of outdated books, with a completely different numbering system.] A partnership may, but is not required to, file a Statement of Partnership with the Superior Court in one or more counties (this is mainly done if real property is owned in the partnership name, to give public notice of the partners' identities.

**Website:** www.legis.state.ga.us/cgi-bin/gl_codes_detail.pl?code=1-1-1

**HAWAII**

**RUPA:** Hawaii Revised Statutes, Title 425, Section 425-101 (H.R.S. 425-101). This contains the basic text of the RUPA, although it is still titled "Uniform Partnership Act."

**Misc.:** Must file registration statement and annual statements with Office of the Director of Commerce and Consumer Affairs (H.R.S. §425-1).

**Website:** www.capitol.hawaii.gov

**NOTE:** *Click on "Archives."*

**IDAHO**

**UPA:** Idaho Code, Title 53, Chapter 3, Part 1, Section 53-3-101 (I.C. §53-3-101). "Uniform Partnership Law."

**Misc.:** Special provisions for mining partnerships found at I.C. §53-401.

**Website:** www3.state.id.us

**NOTE:** *"§" is a symbol for the word section. "§§" is a symbol for the word sections.*

*ILLINOIS*
**UPA:** West's Smith-Hurd Illinois Compiled Statutes Annotated, Chapter 805, Act 205, Article 1 (805 ILCS 205/1). "Uniform Partnership Act." This Act will be repealed effective 1/1/08. Until then, it applies to partnerships formed before 1/1/03 and those formed afterward, if continuing the business of a partnership dissolved pursuant to section 33. A partnership formed before 1/1/03 may elect to be governed by the new Uniform Partnership Act (1997).

**RUPA:** *West's* Smith-Hurd Illinois Compiled Statutes Annotated, Chapter 805, Act 201, Article 1 (805 ILCS 206/1). "Uniform Partnership Act (1997)." Despite its title, this Act contains the basic text of the RUPA. Before 1/1/08, this Act governs partnerships formed after 1/1/03, unless the partnership is continuing the business of a partnership dissolved under the UPA; and governs partnerships formed before 1/1/03 if they so elect. It will govern all partnerships beginning 1/1/08.

**Website:** www.legis.state.il.us

**NOTE:** *Click on "Illinois Compiled Statutes."*

*INDIANA*
**UPA:** West's Annotated Indiana Code, Title 23, Article 4, Chapter 1, Section 1 (A.I.C. §23-4-1-1). "Uniform Partnership Act."

**Website:** www.IN.gov/legislative/ic/code

*IOWA*
**RUPA:** Iowa Code Annotated, Section 486A.101 (I.C.A. §486A.101). This contains the basic text of the RUPA, although it is still titled "Uniform Partnership Act."

**Website:** www2.legis.state.ia.us

**NOTE:** *Click on "Iowa Code."*

*KANSAS*
**RUPA:** Kansas Statutes Annotated—Official, Section 56a-101 (K.S.A. §56a-101). "Kansas Uniform Partnership Act." [There is another set of volumes by a different publisher called *Vernon's Kansas Statutes Annotated,* but it is difficult to locate the partnership laws in this set.]

**Website:** www.kslegislature.org

**NOTE:** *Click on "Statutes."*

**NOTE:** *"§" is a symbol for the word section. "§§" is a symbol for the word sections.*

KENTUCKY          **UPA:** Kentucky Revised Statutes, Chapter 363, Section 150 (K.R.S. §363.150). "Uniform Partnership Act."

**Website:** www.lrc.state.ky.us/statrev/frontpg.htm

LOUISIANA          **UPA/RUPA:** Not adopted by Louisiana.

**Louisiana Partnership Act:** West's LSA Civil Code, Articles 2801 to 2835 (LSA CC 2801). "LSA" stands for "Louisiana Statutes Annotated." Ignore "Title" and "Chapter" numbers. Be sure to find the set of volumes marked "Civil Code," because there are also sets of LSA volumes marked "Revised Statutes," "Civil Procedure," "Criminal Procedure," and various other subjects. Partnerships may be registered with the Secretary of State for a fee of $75. (Obtain form from the Secretary of State if you wish to register.)

**Website:** www.legis.state.la.us

**NOTE:** *Click on "Louisiana Laws."*

MAINE          **UPA:** Maine Revised Statutes Annotated, Title 31, Section 281 (31 M.R.S.A. §281). "Uniform Partnership Act." Ignore "chapter" numbers.

**Website:** http://janus.state.me.us/legis/statutes

MARYLAND          **RUPA:** Annotated Code of Maryland, Corporations & Associations, Section 9-101 (A.C.M., Corp. & Assoc. §9-101). "Maryland Uniform Partnership Act." This act will only remain in effect until 12/31/02. After that date, newly formed partnerships will be governed by the "Maryland Revised Uniform Partnership Act," A.C.M., Corp. & Assoc. §9A-101. Partnerships formed during 2002 have the option of being governed by either act, which should be stated in the partnership agreement. Volumes of the Code of Maryland are arranged by subject, so be sure you have the volume marked "Corporations & Associations."

**Website:** www.mlis.state.md.us

**NOTE:** *Scroll down and click on "Statute text." In the field marked "Enter Article," scroll down and select "Corporations and Associations." In the field marked "Enter Section," type in the section you wish to view (e.g., "9A-101").*

**NOTE:** *"§" is a symbol for the word section. "§§" is a symbol for the word sections.*

MASSACHUSETTS **UPA**: Annotated Laws of Massachusetts, Chapter 108A, Section 1 (A.L.M., c.108A §1). "Uniform Partnership Act."

**Website:** www.state.ma.us/legis/laws/mgl

MICHIGAN **UPA**: Michigan Compiled Laws Annotated, Section 449.1 (M.C.L.A. §449.1). "Uniform Partnership Act." Ignore "volume" and "chapter" numbers.

**NOTE:** *There is a separate set of books titled "Michigan Statutes Annotated," but it is outdated and should not be used.*

**Website:** http://michiganlegislature.org

**NOTE:** *Type "Uniform Partnership Act" in "MCL Full Text Search."*

MINNESOTA **RUPA**: Minnesota Statutes Annotated, Section 323A.1-01 (M.S.A. §323A-1-01). "Uniform Partnership Act (1994)."

**Website:** www.leg.state.mn.us/leg/statutes.asp

MISSISSIPPI **UPA**: Mississippi Code 1971 Annotated, Title 79, Section 79-12-1 (M.C. §79-12-1). "Mississippi Uniform Partnership Law."

**Website:** www.sos.state.ms.us/ed_pubs/mscode

MISSOURI **UPA**: Vernon's Annotated Missouri Statutes, Chapter 358, Section 358.010 (A.M.S. §358.010). "Uniform Partnership Law."

**Website:** www.moga.state.mo.us/homestat.asp

MONTANA **UPA**: Montana Code Annotated 1997, Title 35, Chapter 10, Section 35-10-101 (M.C.A. §35-10-101). "Uniform Partnership Act." Special provisions for mining partnerships found at M.C.A. §35-13-101.

**Website:** www.state.mt.us/govt

**NOTE:** *Click on "Montana Codes, Laws, and Constitution."*

**NOTE:** *"§" is a symbol for the word section. "§§" is a symbol for the word sections.*

NEBRASKA **RUPA**: Revised Statutes of Nebraska, Chapter 67, Section 401 (R.S.N. §67-401). This contains the basic text of the RUPA, although it is titled "Uniform Partnership Act of 1998."

**Website**: http://statutes.unicam.state.ne.us

NEVADA **UPA**: Nevada Revised Statutes Annotated, Chapter 87, Section 87.010 (N.R.S.A. §87.010). "Uniform Partnership Act."

**Website**: www.leg.state.nv.us/NRS/NRSindex

NEW HAMPSHIRE **UPA**: New Hampshire Revised Statutes Annotated 1992, Chapter 304-A, Section 304-A:1 (N.H.R.S.A. §304-A:1). "Uniform Partnership Act." Ignore "Title" numbers; look for "Chapter" numbers.

**Website**: www.state.nh.us/government/laws.html

NEW JERSEY **RUPA**: NJSA (for "New Jersey Statutes Annotated"), Title 42, Chapter 1A, Section 42:1A-1 (N.J.S.A. §42:1A-1). "Uniform Partnership Act (1996)."

**Website**: www.njleg.state.nj.us

**NOTE:** *Scroll down to "Laws and Constitution" and click on "Statutes."*

NEW MEXICO **RUPA**: New Mexico Statutes 1978 Annotated, Chapter 54, Section 54-1A-101 (N.M.S.A. §54-1A-101). "Uniform Partnership Act (1994)."

**Website**: www.state.nm.us

**NOTE:** *Move cursor to "Government in NM" and click on "Laws & Statutes." Then click "Statutes and Constitution of the State of New Mexico."*

NEW YORK **UPA**: McKinney's Consolidated Laws of New York Annotated, Partnership Law, Section 1 (C.L.N.Y., Part. Law §1). "Partnership Law."

**Website**: http://assembly.state.ny.us/leg/?sl=0

NORTH CAROLINA **UPA**: General Statutes of North Carolina, Chapter 59, Section 59-31 (G.S.N.C. §59-31). "Uniform Partnership Act."

**Website**: www.ncga.state.nc.us/Statutes/Statutes.asp

**NOTE:** *"§" is a symbol for the word section. "§§" is a symbol for the word sections.*

NORTH DAKOTA **RUPA:** North Dakota Century Code Annotated, Title 45, Section 45-13-01 (N.D.C.C. §45-13-01).

**Website:** www.state.nd.us/lr/information/statutes/cent-code.html

**NOTE:** *Scroll down and click on "45 Partnerships." Then scroll and click on Chapter "45-13 Partnerships in General."*

OHIO **UPA:** Page's Ohio Revised Code Annotated, Title 17, Section 1775.01 (O.R.C. §1775.01). Titled "Uniform Partnership Law."

**Website:** www.legislature.state.oh.us/laws.cfm

**NOTE:** *Click on "Ohio Revised Code."*

OKLAHOMA **RUPA:** Oklahoma Statutes Annotated, Title 54, Section 1-100 (54 O.S.A. §1-100). "Oklahoma Revised Uniform Partnership Act."

**Website:** www.lsb.state.ok.us

**NOTE:** *Scroll down to "Legislative Information System," then click on "Oklahoma Statutes & Constitution."*

OREGON **RUPA:** Oregon Revised Statutes Annotated, Chapter 67, Section 67.005 (O.R.S. §67.005). "Oregon Revised Partnership Act."

**Website:** www.leg.state.or.us/ors

PENNSYLVANIA **UPA:** Purdon's Pennsylvania Consolidated Statutes Annotated, Title 15, Section 8301. (15 Pa.C.S.A. §8301). "Uniform Partnership Act."

**Misc.:** 15 Pa.C.S.A. §8101, called "Partnership Code," contains general partnership provisions not found in the UPA.

**Website:** http://members.aol.com/StatutesPA/15.Cp.83.html

**NOTE:** *No state-provided online statutes database.*

**NOTE:** *"§" is a symbol for the word section. "§§" is a symbol for the word sections.*

RHODE ISLAND    **UPA:** General Laws of Rhode Island, Section 7-12-12 (G.L.R.I. §7-12-12). "Uniform Partnership Act." Ignore "Title" and "Chapter" numbers.

**Misc.:** G.L.R.I §7-12-1 contains additional partnership provisions not found in the UPA.

**Website:** www.rilin.state.ri.us/statutes/statutes.html

**NOTE:** *Scroll down and click on "7 Corporations, Associations and Partnerships," then scroll down and click on "CHAPTER 7-12 Partnerships."*

SOUTH
CAROLINA
    **UPA:** Code of Laws of South Carolina, Title 33, Section 33-41-10 (C.L.S.C. §33-41-10). "Uniform Partnership Act."

**Website:** www.lpitr.state.sc.us/code/statmast.htm

**NOTE:** *Scroll down and click on "Title 33 - Corporations, Partnerships and Associations." Then scroll down and click on "Uniform Partnership Act."*

SOUTH DAKOTA    **RUPA:** South Dakota Codified Laws, Title 48, Chapter 7A, Section 48-7A-101 (S.D.C.L. §48-7A-101). "Uniform Partnership Act."

**Website:** http://legis.state.sd.us

**NOTE:** *Click on "Codified Laws."*

TENNESSEE    **RUPA:** Tennessee Code Annotated, Title 61, Section 61-1-101 (T.C.A. §61-1-101). "Revised Uniform Partnership Act."

**Website:** www.tennesseeanytime.org/laws/laws.html

**NOTE:** *Click on "Tennessee Code and Constitution," then click on + sign before "Tennessee Code," which will bring up a list of titles. Then scroll down and click on "TITLE 61 PARTNERSHIPS," then click on "1. Revised Uniform Partnership Act."*

**NOTE:** *"§" is a symbol for the word section. "§§" is a symbol for the word sections.*

**TEXAS**  **RUPA**: Vernon's Texas Civil Statutes, Article 6132b (T.C.S.A., Art. 6132b). "Texas Revised Partnership Act." The Texas laws are divided into subjects, so be sure you have a volume marked "Civil Statutes."

**Website**: www.capitol.state.tx.us/statutes/statutes.html

**NOTE:** *Scroll down and click on "Vernon's Texas Civil Statutes." Then scroll down to "Title 105. Partnerships and Joint Stock Companies" and click on "CHAPTER ONE PARTNERSHIPS."*

**UTAH**  **UPA**: Utah Code Annotated 1953, Title 48, Section 48-1-1 (U.C.A. §48-1-1). Titled "General and Limited Liability Partnerships."

**Website**: www.le.state.ut.us/~code/code.htm

**NOTE:** *Scroll down and click on "Title 48 Partnership." Then click on "Title 48 Chapter 01 General and Limited Liability Partnerships."*

**VERMONT**  **RUPA**: Vermont Statutes Annotated, Title 11, Section 3201 (11 V.S.A. §3201). Titled "Partnerships."

**Website**: www.leg.state.vt.us/statutes/statutes2.htm

**NOTE:** *Scroll down and click on "TITLE 11. Corporations, Partnerships and Associations," then click on "22. Partnerships."*

**VIRGINIA**  **RUPA**: Code of Virginia 1950, Title 50, Section 50-73.79 (C.V. §50-73.79). "Virginia Uniform Partnership Act." Ignore "Chapter" numbers; look for "Title" and "Section" numbers.

**Misc.**: C.V. §50-74 contains filing requirements.

**Website**: http://leg1.state.va.us

**NOTE:** *Click on "Code of Virginia." Then click on "Table of Contents" and scroll down and click on "Title 50 Partnerships." Then click on "Chapter 2.2 Virginia Uniform Partnership Act."*

**NOTE:** *"§" is a symbol for the word section. "§§" is a symbol for the word sections.*

*WASHINGTON*    **RUPA:** West's Revised Code of Washington Annotated, Title 25, Chapter 25.05, Section 25.05.005 (R.C.W.A. §25.05.005). "Revised Uniform Partnership Act."

                **Website:** www.leg.wa.gov/rcw/index.cfm

                **NOTE:** *Click on "RCW by title," then scroll down and click on "Title 25-Partnerships." Then click on "25.05 Revised uniform partnership act."*

*WEST VIRGINIA*   **RUPA:** West Virginia Code, Chapter 47B, Article 1, Section 47B-1-1 (W.V.C. §47B-1-1). "Uniform Partnership Act."

                **Website:** www.legis.state.wv.us/legishp.html

                **NOTE:** *Click on "WV Code," then click on "State Code." Using the "Select Chapter" drop down menu, scroll to "Chapter 47B Uniform Partnership Act."*

*WISCONSIN*     **UPA:** West's Wisconsin Statutes Annotated, Section 178.01 (W.S.A. §178.01). "Uniform Partnership Act." Ignore "Chapter" numbers.

                **Website:** www.legis.state.wi.us/rsb/stats.html

                **NOTE:** *Click on "The Updated Wisconsin Statutes & Annotations," then scroll down and click on "Chapter 178."*

*WYOMING*      **RUPA:** Wyoming Statutes Annotated, Title 17, Chapter 21, Section 17-21-101 (W.S.A. §17-21-101). "Uniform Partnership Act."

                **Website:** http://legisweb.state.wy.us/statutes/statutes.htm

                **NOTE:** *Scroll down and click on "Title 17 Corporations, Partnerships and Associations," then scroll down to "Chapter 21 - Uniform Partnership Act" and click on the desired provision.*

# APPENDIX B: PARTNERSHIP ACTS

This appendix contains: (1) the full text of the Uniform Partnership Act (UPA); (2) the full text of the Revised Uniform Partnership Act (RUPA); and, (3) the full text of the Louisiana Partnership Act (as Louisiana has not adopted either the UPA or the RUPA).

Each state that has adopted the UPA or the RUPA has made revisions to the basic Act. All of the states have assigned their own section number to the provisions, based on the state's statute numbering system. The most typical revisions range from minor changes (such as using the word "part" instead of "act," changing the order of the various provisions, or adding, deleting, or changing definitions), to major rewrites of certain provisions. Your state legislature may also change the partnership laws at any time. Therefore, it is important that you read the Partnership Act as it was adopted and changed by your state. See Chapter 3 for more information about locating your state's partnership laws at your local library or law library, as well as the information under your state's listing in Appendix A. Finally, more and more states are abandoning the UPA and adopting the RUPA.

**NOTE:** *"§" is a symbol for the word section, which may also be abbreviated "s".*

# Uniform Partnership Act

On the following pages is the Uniform Partnership Act (UPA) in its basic form. At the time of publication, the UPA was in effect in the following states:

| | | | |
|---|---|---|---|
| Arkansas* | Kansas | Missouri | North Carolina |
| Delaware | Kentucky | Montana | Ohio |
| Georgia | Maine | Nevada | Pennsylvania |
| Idaho | Massachusetts | New Hampshire | Rhode Island |
| Indiana | Michigan | New Jersey | South Carolina |
| Illinois** | Mississippi | New York | Utah |

\* The RUPA is being phased in and goes into effect in full on 1/1/05.
\*\* The RUPA is being phased in and goes into effect in full on 1/1/08.

The newer, Revised Uniform Partnership Act (RUPA) is being adopted by more states each year. Therefore, if your state is listed above, you may want to check at your local library or law library to be sure your state has not recently changed to the RUPA.

## Contents

Section 1. Name of act.
Section 2. Definition of terms.
Section 3. Interpretation of knowledge and notice.
Section 4. Rules of construction.
Section 5. Rules for cases not provided for in this act.
Section 6. "Partnership" defined.
Section 7. Rules for determining the existence of a partnership.
Section 8. Partnership property.
Section 9. Partner agent of partnership as to partnership business.
Section 10. Conveyance of real property of the partnership.
Section 11. Partnership bound by admission of partner.
Section 12. Partnership charged with knowledge of or notice to partner.
Section 13. Partnership bound by partner's wrongful act.
Section 14. Partnership bound by partner's breach of trust.
Section 15. Nature of partner's liability.
Section 16. Partner by estoppel.
Section 17. Liability of incoming partner.
Section 18. Rules determining rights and duties of partners.

Section 19. Partnership books.
Section 20. Duty of partners to render information.
Section 21. Partner accountable as a fiduciary.
Section 22. Right to an account.
Section 23. Continuation of partnership beyond fixed term.
Section 24. Extent of property rights of a partner.
Section 25. Nature of a partner's right in specific partnership property.
Section 26. Nature of partner's interest in the partnership.
Section 27. Assignment of partner's interest.
Section 28. Partner's interest subject to charging order.
Section 29. "Dissolution" defined.
Section 30. Partnership not terminated by dissolution.
Section 31. Causes of dissolution.
Section 32. Dissolution by decree of court.
Section 33. General effect of dissolution on authority of partner.
Section 34. Right of partner to contribution from copartners after dissolution.
Section 35. Power of partner to bind partnership to third persons after dissolution.
Section 36. Effect of dissolution on partner's existing liability.

**Section 1.    Name of act.**

This act may be cited as the "Uniform Partnership Act."

**Section 2.    Definition of terms.**

In this act:

(1) "Court" means every court and judge having jurisdiction in the action.

(2) "Business" means every trade, occupation, or profession.

(3) "Person" means individuals, partnerships, corporations, and other associations.

(4) "Bankrupt" means a bankrupt under the Federal Bankruptcy Act or an insolvent person under any state insolvency act.

(5) "Conveyance" means every assignment, lease, mortgage, or encumbrance.

(6) "Real property" means land and any interest or estate in land.

**Section 3.    Interpretation of knowledge and notice.**

In this act:

(1) A person has "knowledge" of a fact not only when he has actual knowledge of it, but also when he has knowledge of such other facts as in the circumstances show bad faith.

(2) A person has "notice" of a fact when another person claiming the benefit of the notice:

    (a)  States the fact to the person, or

    (b)  Delivers through the mail or by other means of communication a written statement of the fact to the person or to his agent at his place of business or residence.

**Section 4.    Rules of construction.**

(1) The rule that statutes in derogation of the common law are to be strictly construed shall have no application to this act.

(2) The law of estoppel and of agency shall apply under this act.

(3) This act shall be so interpreted and construed as to make uniform the law of those states that enact it.

(4) This act shall not be construed to impair the obligation of any contract existing when the act goes into effect, nor to affect any action or proceedings begun or right that has accrued before this act takes effect.

**Section 5.    Rules for cases not provided for in this act.**

In any case not provided for in this act, the rules of law and equity, including the law merchant, shall govern.

**Section 6.    "Partnership" defined.**

(1) A "partnership" is an association of two or more persons to carry on a business for profit as coowners.

(2) An association formed under any other statute of this state, or any statute adopted by authority other than the authority of this state, is not a partnership under this act, unless the association would have been a partnership in this state before the adoption of this act. This act shall apply to limited partnerships except insofar as the statutes relating to limited partnerships are inconsistent with this act.

**Section 7.    Rules for determining the existence of a partnership.**

In determining whether a partnership exists, these rules shall apply:

(1) Except as provided by §16, persons who are not partners as to each other are not partners as to third persons.

(2) Joint tenancy, tenancy in common, tenancy by the entireties, joint property, common property, or part ownership of itself does not establish a partnership whether the coowners do or do not share any profits made by the use of the property.

(3) The sharing of gross returns of itself does not establish a partnership, whether the persons sharing them do or do not have a joint or common right or interest in any property from which the returns are derived.

(4) The receipt by a person of a share of the profits of a business is prima facie evidence that he is a partner in the business, but no such inference shall be drawn if the profits were received in payment:

    (a) Of a debt by installments or otherwise;

    (b) As wages of an employee or rent to a landlord;

    (c) As an annuity to a widow or representative of a deceased partner;

    (d) As interest on a loan, though the amount of payment varies with the profits of the business; or

    (e) As the consideration for the sale of goodwill of a business or other property by installments or otherwise.

### Section 8. Partnership property.

(1) All property originally brought into the partnership or subsequently acquired by purchase or otherwise on account of the partnership is partnership property.

(2) Unless a contrary intention appears, property acquired with partnership funds is partnership property.

(3) Any estate in real property may be acquired in the partnership name. Title so acquired can only be conveyed only in the partnership name.

(4) A conveyance to a partnership in the partnership name, though without words of inheritance, passes the entire estate of the grantor, unless a contrary intent appears.

### Section 9. Partner agent of partnership as to partnership business.

(1) Every partner is an agent of the partnership for the purpose of its business. The act of every partner including the execution in the partnership name of any instrument, for apparently carrying on in the usual way the business of the partnership of which he is a member, binds the partnership, unless the partner so acting has in fact no authority to act for the partnership in the particular matter, and the person with whom he is dealing has knowledge of the fact that he has no authority.

(2) An act of a partner that is not apparently for the carrying on of the business of the partnership in the usual way does not bind the partnership unless authorized by the other partners.

(3) Unless authorized by the other partners or unless they have abandoned the business, one or more but less than all the partners have no authority to:

    (a) Assign the partnership property in trust for creditors or on the assignee's promise to pay the debts of the partnership,

    (b) Dispose of the goodwill of the business,

    (c) Do any other act that would make it impossible to carry on the ordinary business of a partnership,

    (d) Confess a judgment,

    (e) Submit a partnership claim or liability to arbitration or reference.

(4) No act of a partner in contravention of a restriction on authority shall bind the partnership to persons

### Section 10. Conveyance of real property of the partnership.

(1) When title to real property is in the partnership name, any partner may convey title to the property by a conveyance executed in the partnership name; but the partnership may recover the property unless the partner's act binds the partnership under the provisions of §9(1) or unless the purchaser or his assignee is a holder for value without knowledge that the partner has exceeded his authority in making the conveyance.

(2) Where title to real property is in the name of the partnership, a conveyance executed by a partner, in his own name, passes the equitable interest of the partnership, provided the act is one within the authority of the partner under the provisions of §9(1).

(3) When title to real property is in the name of one or more, but not all, of the partners, and the public records do not disclose the right of the partnership, the partners in whose name the title stands may convey title to the property, but the partnership may recover the property if the partners' act does not bind the partnership under the provisions of §9(1) unless the purchaser or his assignee is a holder for value without knowledge that the partners have exceeded their authority in making the conveyance.

(4) Where the title to real property is in the name of one or more or all the partners, or in a third person in trust for the partnership, a conveyance executed by a partner in the partnership name, or in his own name, passes the equitable interest of the partnership, provided the act is one within the authority of the partner under the provisions of §9(1).

(5)  When the title to real property is in the names of all the partners, a conveyance executed by all the partners passes all their rights in such property.

### Section 11.    Partnership bound by admission of partner.

An admission or representation made by any partner concerning partnership affairs within the scope of his authority as conferred by this act is evidence against the partnership.

### Section 12.    Partnership charged with knowledge of or notice to partner.

Notice to any partner of a matter concerning partnership affairs, and the knowledge of the partner acting in the particular matter, acquired while a partner or then present to his mind, and the knowledge of any other partner who reasonably could and should have communicated it to the acting partner, operate as notice to or knowledge of the partnership, except in the case of a fraud on the partnership committed by or with the consent of that partner.

### Section 13.    Partnership bound by partner's wrongful act.

When loss or injury is caused to a person, not a partner in the partnership, or any penalty is incurred by a wrongful act or omission of a partner acting in the ordinary course of the business of the partnership or with the authority of his copartners, the partnership is liable for it to the same extent as the partner so acting or omitting to act.

### Section 14.    Partnership bound by partner's breach of trust.

The partnership is bound to make good the loss:
(1)  When one partner acting within the scope of his apparent authority receives money or property of a third person and misapplies it; and
(2)  When the partnership in the course of its business receives money or property of a third person and the money or property so received is misapplied by a partner while it is in the custody of the partnership.

### Section 15.    Nature of partner's liability.

All partners are liable:
(1 )  Jointly and severally for everything chargeable to the partnership under §§13 and 14.
(2)  Jointly for all other debts and obligations of the partnership; but a partner may enter into a separate obligation to perform a partnership contract.

### Section 16.    Partner by estoppel.

(1)  When a person, by words spoken or written or by conduct, represents himself, or consents to another representing him to anyone, as a partner in an existing partnership or with one or more persons not actual partners, he is liable to any person to whom the representation has been made, who has given credit on the faith of the representation to the actual or apparent partnership, and if he has made the representation or consented to it being made in a public manner, he is liable to the person, whether the representation has or has not been made or communicated to the person giving credit by or with the knowledge of the apparent partner making the representation or consenting to its being made.
(a)  When a partnership liability results, he is liable as though he were an actual member of the partnership.
(b)  When no partnership liability results, he is liable jointly with the other persons, if any, so consenting to the contract or representation as to incur liability; otherwise he is liable separately.
(2)  When a person has been thus represented to be partner in an existing partnership, or with one or more persons not actual partners, he is an agent of the persons consenting to the representation to bind them to the same extent and in the same manner as though he were a partner with respect to persons who rely upon the representation. When all members of the existing partnership consent to the representation, a partnership act or obligation results; but otherwise it is the joint act or obligation of the person acting and the persons consenting to the representation.

### Section 17.    Liability of incoming partner.

A person admitted as a partner into an existing partnership is liable for all the obligations of the partnership arising before his admission as though he had been a partner when the obligations were incurred, except that this liability shall be satisfied only out of partnership property.

**Section 18.      Rules determining rights and duties of partners.**

The rights and duties of the partners in relation to the partnership shall be determined, subject to any agreement between them, by the following rules:

(1)   Each partner shall be repaid his contributions, whether by way of capital or advances, to the partnership property, and shall share equally in the profits and surplus remaining after all liabilities, including those to partners, are satisfied; and must contribute toward the losses, whether of capital or otherwise, sustained by the partnership according to his share in the profits.

(2)   The partnership must indemnify every partner for payments made and personal liabilities reasonably incurred by him in the ordinary and proper conduct of its business or for the preservation of its business or property.

(3)   A partner who in aid of the partnership makes any payment or advance beyond the amount of capital that he agreed to contribute shall be paid interest from the date of the payment or advance.

(4)   A partner shall receive interest on the capital contributed by him from the date when repayment should be made.

(5)   All partners have equal rights in the management and conduct of the partnership business.

(6)   No partner is entitled to remuneration for acting in the partnership business, except that a surviving partner is entitled to reasonable compensation for his services in winding up the partnership affairs.

(7)   No person can become a member of a partnership without the consent of all the partners.

(8)   Any difference arising about ordinary matters connected with the partnership business may be decided by a majority of the partners; but no act in contravention of any agreement between the partners may be done rightfully without the consent of all the partners.

**Section 19.      Partnership books.**

The partnership books shall be kept, subject to any agreement between the partners, at the principal place of business of the partnership, and every partner shall have access to and may inspect and copy any of them at all times.

**Section 20.      Duty of partners to render information.**

On demand partners shall render true and full information of all things affecting the partnership to any partner or the legal representative of any deceased partner or partner under legal disability.

**Section 21.      Partner accountable as a fiduciary.**

(1)   Every partner must account to the partnership for any benefit, and hold as trustee for it any profits, derived by him without the consent of the other partners from any transaction connected with the formation, conduct, or liquidation of the partnership or from any use by him of its property.

(2)   This section applies also to the representatives of a deceased partner engaged in the liquidation of the affairs of the partnership as the personal representatives of the last surviving partner.

**Section 22.      Right to an account.**

Any partner shall have the right to a formal account of partnership affairs:

(1)   If he is wrongfully excluded from the partnership business or possession of its property by his co-partners.

(2)   If the right exists under the terms of an agreement.

(3)   As provided by §21.

(4)   Whenever other circumstances render it just and reasonable.

**Section 23.      Continuation of partnership beyond fixed term.**

(1)   When a partnership for a fixed term or particular undertaking is continued after the termination of the term or undertaking without an express agreement, the rights and duties of the partners remain the same as they were at termination so far as is consistent with a partnership at will.

(2)   A continuation of the business by the partners or such of them as habitually acted in it during the term without any settlement or liquidation of the partnership affairs is prima facie evidence of a continuation of the partnership.

**Section 24.      Extent of property rights of a partner.**

The property rights of a partner are:

(1)   His rights in specific partnership property;

(2)   His interest in the partnership; and

(3)   His right to participate in the management.

**Section 25.  Nature of a partner's right in specific partnership property.**
(1)  A partner is co-owner with his partners of specific partnership property holding as a tenant in partnership.
(2)  The incidents of this tenancy are such that:
  (a)  Subject to the provisions of this act and to any agreement between the partners, a partner has an equal right with his partners to possess specific partnership property for partnership purposes; but he has no right to possess the property for any other purpose without the consent of his partners.
  (b)  A partner's right in specific partnership property is not assignable except in connection with the assignment of rights of all the partners in the same property.
  (c)  A partner's right in specific partnership property is not subject to attachment or execution, except on a claim against the partnership. When partnership property is attached for a partnership debt, the partners, or any of them, or the representatives of a deceased partner, cannot claim any right under the homestead or exemption laws.
  (d)  On the death of a partner his right in specific partnership property vests in the surviving partner or partners, except when the deceased was the last surviving partner, his right in the property vests in his legal representative. The surviving partner or partners or the legal representative of the last surviving partner has no right to possess the partnership property except for a partnership purpose.
  (e)  A partner's right in specific partnership property is not subject to dower, curtesy, or allowances to widows, heirs, or next of kin.

**Section 26.  Nature of partner's interest in the partnership.**
A partner's interest in the partnership is his share of the profits and surplus. It is personal property.

**Section 27.  Assignment of partner's interest.**
(1)  A conveyance by a partner of his interest in the partnership of itself does not dissolve the partnership, nor, as against the other partners in the absence of agreement, entitle the assignee, during the continuance of the partnership to interfere in the management or administration of the partnership business or affairs, to require any information or account of partnership transactions, or to inspect the partnership books; but it merely entitles the assignee to receive in accordance with his contract the profits to which the assigning partner would otherwise be entitled.
(2)  If the partnership is dissolved, the assignee is entitled to receive his assignor's interest and may require an account from the date only of the last account agreed to by all the partners.

**Section 28.  Partner's interest subject to charging order.**
(1)  On application to a court having jurisdiction by any judgment creditor of a partner, the court may charge the interest of the debtor partner with payment of the unsatisfied amount of the judgment with interest, and may then or later appoint a receiver of his share of the profits and of any other money due or to become due to him from the partnership, and make all other orders to take the actions that the debtor partner might have made or that the circumstances of the case may require.
(2)  The partner's interest charged may be redeemed at any time before foreclosure, or, in case of a sale being directed by the court, may be purchased without thereby causing a dissolution:
  (a)  With separate property by any one or more of the partners; or
  (b)  With partnership property by any one or more of the partners with the consent of all the partners whose interests are not charged or sold.
(3)  Nothing in this act shall deprive a partner of any right under the exemption laws covering his interest in the partnership.

**Section 29.  "Dissolution" defined.**
The "dissolution" of a partnership is the change in the relation of the partners caused by a partner ceasing to be associated in the carrying on, as distinguished from the winding up, of the business.

**Section 30.  Partnership not terminated by dissolution.**
On dissolution the partnership is not terminated, but continues until the winding up of partnership affairs is completed.

### Section 31.   Causes of dissolution.

Dissolution is caused:

(1)  Without violation of the agreement between the partners:

    (a)  By the termination of the definite term or particular undertaking specified in the agreement,

    (b)  By the expressed decision of a partner when no definite term or particular undertaking is specified,

    (c)  By the express will of all the partners who have not assigned their interests or suffered them to be charged for their separate debts, either before or after the termination of any specified term or particular undertaking, or

    (d)  By the expulsion of a partner from the business bona fide in accordance with such a power conferred by the agreement between the partners;

(2)  In contravention of the agreement between the partners when the circumstances do not permit a dissolution under any other provision of this section by the expressed decision of a partner at any time;

(3)  By any event that makes it unlawful for the business of the partnership to be carried on or for the members to carry it on in partnership;

(4)  By the death of any partner;

(5)  By the bankruptcy of a partner or the partnership;

(6)  By judgment of court under §32.

### Section 32.   Dissolution by decree of court.

The court shall adjudge a dissolution:

(1)  On application by or for a partner when:

    (a)  A partner has been adjudicated mentally incompetent or is shown to be of unsound mind.

    (b)  A partner becomes in any other way incapable of performing his part of the partnership contract.

    (c)  A partner has been guilty of conduct that tends to affect prejudicially the carrying on of the business.

    (d)  A partner willfully or persistently commits a breach of the partnership agreement, or otherwise so conducts himself in matters relating to the partnership business that it is not reasonably practicable to carry on the business in partnership with him.

    (e)  The business of the partnership can only be carried on at a loss.

    (f)  Other circumstances render a dissolution equitable.

(2)  On the application of the purchaser of a partner's interest under §§27 and 28:

    (a)  After the termination of the specified term or particular undertaking.

    (b)  At any time if the partnership was a partnership at will when the interest was assigned or when the charging order was issued.

### Section 33.   General effect of dissolution on authority of partner.

Except as may be necessary to wind up partnership affairs or to complete transactions begun but not then finished, dissolution terminates all authority of a partner to act for the partnership:

(1)  With respect to the partners when the dissolution is not by the act, bankruptcy, or death of a partner; or when the dissolution is by the act, bankruptcy, or death of a partner when §34 so requires.

(2)  With respect to persons not partners, as declared in §35.

### Section 34.   Right of partner to contribution from co-partners after dissolution.

When the dissolution is caused by the act, death, or bankruptcy of a partner, each partner is liable to his co-partners for his share of any liability created by a partner acting for the partnership as if the partnership had not been dissolved unless:

(1)  The dissolution being by act of a partner, the partner acting for the partnership had knowledge of the dissolution, or

(2)  The dissolution being by the death or bankruptcy of a partner, the partner acting for the partnership had knowledge or notice of the death or bankruptcy.

### Section 35.   Power of partner to bind partnership to third persons after dissolution.

(1)  After dissolution a partner can bind the partnership except as provided in subsection (3):

    (a)  By an act appropriate for winding up partnership affairs or completing transactions unfinished at dissolution;

    (b)  By a transaction that would bind the partnership if dissolution had not taken place, provided the other party to the transaction:

1.  Had extended credit to the partnership before dissolution and had no knowledge or notice of the dissolution, or
2.  Though he had not extended credit, had nevertheless known of the partnership before dissolution and, having no knowledge or notice of dissolution, the fact of dissolution had not been advertised in a newspaper of general circulation in the place or in each place, if more than one, at which the partnership business was regularly carried on.

(2) The liability of a partner under subsection (1)(b) shall be satisfied out of partnership assets alone when before dissolution that partner had been:

(a)  Unknown as a partner to the person with whom the contract is made; and

(b)  So far unknown and inactive in partnership affairs that the business reputation of the partnership could not be said to have been in any degree due to his connection with it.

(3) The partnership is in no case bound by an act of a partner after dissolution:

(a)  When the partnership is dissolved because it is unlawful to carry on the business, unless the act is appropriate for winding up partnership affairs;

(b)  When the partner has become bankrupt; or

(c)  When the partner has no authority to wind up partnership affairs; except by a transaction with one who:

1.  Had extended credit to the partnership before dissolution and had no knowledge or notice of his want of authority; or
2.  Had not extended credit to the partnership before dissolution, and, having no knowledge or notice of his want of authority, the fact of his want of authority had not been advertised in the manner provided for advertising the fact of dissolution in subsection (1)(b)2.

(4) Nothing in this section shall affect the liability of a person under §16 who after dissolution represents himself or consents to another representing him as a partner in a partnership engaged in carrying on business.

## Section 36.    Effect of dissolution on partner's existing liability.

(1) The dissolution of the partnership of itself does not discharge the existing liability of any partner.

(2) A partner is discharged from any existing liability upon dissolution of the partnership by an agreement to that effect between himself, the partnership creditor and the person or partnership continuing the business. The agreement may be inferred from the course of dealing between the creditor having knowledge of the dissolution and the person or partnership continuing the business.

(3) When a person agrees to assume the existing obligations of a dissolved partnership, the partners whose obligations have been assumed shall be discharged from any liability to any creditor of the partnership who, knowing of the agreement, consents to a material alteration in the nature or time of payment of the obligations.

(4) The individual property of a deceased partner shall be liable for all obligations of the partnership incurred while he was a partner but subject to the prior payment of his separate debts.

## Section 37.    Right to wind up.

Unless otherwise agreed the partners who have not wrongfully dissolved the partnership or the legal representative of the last surviving partner, not bankrupt, has the right to wind up the partnership affairs; but any partner, his legal representative or his assignee may obtain winding up by the court.

## Section 38.    Rights of partners to application of partnership property.

(1) When dissolution is caused in any way except in contravention of the partnership agreement, each partner as against his copartners and all persons claiming through them, unless otherwise agreed, may have the partnership property applied to discharge its liabilities and the surplus applied to pay in cash the net amount owing to the respective partners. If dissolution is caused by the bona fide expulsion of a partner under the partnership agreement and if the expelled partner is discharged from all partnership liabilities either by payment or agreement under §36(2), he shall receive in cash only the net amount due him from the partnership.

(2) When dissolution is caused in contravention of the partnership agreement, the rights of the partners shall be as follows:

(a)  Each partner who has not caused dissolution wrongfully shall have:

1.  All the rights specified in subsection (1), and
2.  The right to damages for breach of the agreement against each partner who has caused the dissolution wrongfully.

(b) If all the partners who have not wrongfully caused the dissolution desire to continue the business in the same name, either by themselves or jointly with others, they may do so during the agreed term for the partnership and for that purpose may possess the partnership property, if they secure the payment by bond approved by the court or pay the value of his interest in the partnership at the dissolution to a partner who has caused the dissolution wrongfully, less any damages recoverable under subsection (2)(a)2., and in like manner indemnify him against all present or future partnership liabilities.

(c) A partner who has caused the dissolution wrongfully shall have:
   1. If the business is not continued under the provisions of subsection (2)(b), all the rights of a partner under subsection (1), subject to subsection (2)(a)2.
   2. If the business is continued under subsection (2)(b), the right, as against his copartners and all claiming through them in respect of their interests in the partnership, to have the value of his interest in the partnership less any damages caused to his copartners by the dissolution, ascertained and paid to him in cash or the payment secured by bond approved by the court, and to be released from all existing liabilities of the partnership; but in ascertaining the value of the partner's interest, the value of the good will of the business shall not be considered.

**Section 39.    Rights when partnership is dissolved for fraud or misrepresentation.**
When a partnership contract is rescinded on the ground of the fraud or misrepresentation of one of the parties to it, the party entitled to rescind is, without prejudice to any other right, entitled:

(1) To a lien on, or a right of retention of, the surplus of the partnership property after satisfying the partnership liabilities to third persons for any sum of money paid by him for the purchase of an interest in the partnership and for capital or advances contributed by him; and

(2) After all liabilities to third persons have been satisfied to stand in the place of the creditors of the partnership for payments made by him for partnership liabilities; and

(3) To be indemnified by the person guilty of the fraud or making the representation against all debts and liabilities of the partnership.

**Section 40.    Rules for distribution.**
In settling accounts between the partners after dissolution, the following rules shall be observed, subject to any agreement to the contrary:

(1) The assets of the partnership are:
   (a) The partnership property,
   (b) The contributions of the partners necessary for the payment of all the liabilities specified in subsection (4).

(2) The liabilities of the partnership shall rank in order of payment, as follows:
   (a) Those owing to creditors other than partners,
   (b) Those owing to partners other than for capital and profits,
   (c) Those owing to partners for capital,
   (d) Those owing to partners for profits.

(3) The assets shall be applied in the order of their declaration in subsection (1) to the satisfaction of the liabilities.

(4) As provided by §18(a), the partners shall contribute the amount necessary to satisfy the liabilities; but if any, but not all, of the partners are insolvent or, not being subject to process, refuse to contribute, the other partners shall contribute their share of the liabilities and, in the relative proportions in which they share the profits, the additional amount necessary to pay the liabilities.

(5) An assignee for the benefit of creditors or any person appointed by the court may enforce the contributions specified in subsection (4).

(6) Any partner or his legal representative may enforce the contributions specified in subsection (4) to the extent of the amount that he has paid in excess of his share of the liability.

(7) The individual property of a deceased partner shall be liable for the contributions specified in sub-section (4).

(8) When partnership property and the individual properties of the partners are in possession of a court for distribution, partnership creditors shall have priority on partnership property and separate creditors on individual property, saving the rights of lien or secured creditors as heretofore provided.

(9) When a partner has become bankrupt or his estate is insolvent, the claims against his separate property shall rank in the following order:
   (a) Those owing to separate creditors,

 (b) Those owing to partnership creditors.

 (c) Those owing to partners by way of contribution.

### Section 41. Liability of persons continuing the business in certain cases.

(1) When a new partner is admitted into an existing partnership, or a partner retires and assigns, or the representative of the deceased partner assigns, his rights in partnership property to two or more of the partners, or to one or more of the partners and one or more third persons, and the business is continued without liquidation of the partnership affairs, creditors of the first or dissolved partnership are also creditors of the partnership continuing the business.

(2) When all but one partner retire and assign, or the representative of a deceased partner assigns, their rights in partnership property to the remaining partner who continues the business without liquidation of partnership affairs, either alone or with others, creditors of the dissolved partnership are also creditors of the person or partnership continuing the business.

(3) When any partner retires or dies and the business of the dissolved partnership is continued as set forth in subsections (1) and (2) with the consent of the retired partners or the representative of the deceased partner, but without any assignment of his right in partnership property, rights of creditors of the dissolved partnership and of the creditors of the person or partnership continuing the business shall be the same as if the assignment had been made.

(4) When all the partners or their representatives assign their rights in partnership property to one or more third persons who promise to pay the debts and who continue the business of the dissolved partnership, creditors of the dissolved partnership are also creditors.

(5) When any partner wrongfully causes a dissolution and the remaining partners continue the business under the provisions of §38(2)(b), either alone or with others, and without liquidation of the partnership affairs, creditors of the dissolved partnership are also creditors of the person or partnership continuing the business.

(6) When a partner is expelled and the remaining partners continue the business, either alone or with others without liquidation of the partnership affairs, creditors of the dissolved partnership are also creditors of the person or partnership continuing the business.

(7) The liability of a third person becoming a partner in the partnership continuing the business under this section to the creditors of the dissolved partnership shall be satisfied out of partnership property only.

(8) When the business of a partnership after dissolution is continued under any conditions set forth in this section, the creditors of the dissolved partnership, as against the separate creditors of the retiring or deceased partner or the representative of the deceased partner, have a prior right to any claim of the retired partner or the representative of the deceased partner against the person or partnership continuing the business on account of the retired or deceased partner's interest in the dissolved partnership or on account of any consideration promised for the interest or for his right in partnership property.

(9) Nothing in this section shall modify any right of creditors to set aside an assignment on the ground of fraud .

(10) The use by the person or partnership continuing the business of the partnership name, or the name of a deceased partner as part of it of itself shall not make the individual property of the deceased partner liable for any debts contracted by the person or partnership.

### Section 42. Rights of retiring partner or estate of deceased partner when the business is continued.

When a partner retires or dies and the business is continued under any of the conditions set forth in §41(1, 2, 3, 4, 5, 6) or §38(2)(b), without any settlement of accounts between him or his estate and the person or partnership continuing the business, unless otherwise agreed, he or his legal representative, as against the persons or partnership, may have the value of his interest at the date of dissolution ascertained, and shall receive as an ordinary creditor an amount equal to the value of his interest in the dissolved partnership with interest or, at his option or that of his legal representative, instead of interest, the profits attributable to the use of his right in the property of the dissolved partnership; but the creditors of the dissolved partnership as against the separate creditors, or the representative of the retired or deceased partner, shall have priority on any claim arising under this section, as provided by §41(8).

### Section 43. Accrual of actions.

The right to an account of his interest shall accrue to any partner or his legal representative as against the winding up partners or the surviving partners or the person or partnership continuing the business at the date of dissolution in the absence of any agreement to the contrary.

# Revised Uniform Partnership Act

On the following pages is the Revised Uniform Partnership Act (RUPA) in its basic form. At the time of publication, the RUPA had been adopted by the following states:

| | | | |
|---|---|---|---|
| Alabama | District of Columbia | Nebraska | Texas |
| Alaska | Florida | New Mexico | Vermont |
| Arizona | Hawaii | North Dakota | Virginia |
| Arkansas* | Illinois** | Oklahoma | Washington |
| California | Iowa | Oregon | West Virginia |
| Colorado | Maryland | South Dakota | Wyoming |
| Connecticut | Minnesota | Tennessee | |

\* The RUPA is being phased in and goes into effect in full on 1/1/05.
\*\* The RUPA is being phased in and goes into effect in full on 1/1/08.

The RUPA is being adopted by more states each year. Therefore, if your state is *not* listed above, you may want to check at your local library or law library to be sure your state has not recently changed to the RUPA.

## Contents

**Section 1.  Uniformity of application and construction.**

This act shall be applied and construed to effectuate its general purpose to make uniform the law with respect to the subject of this act.

**Section 2.  Short title.**

This act may be cited as the Revised Uniform Partnership Act.

**Section 3.  Definitions.**

As provided in this act:

(1) "Act" means the Revised Uniform Partnership Act.

(2) "Business" means every trade, occupation, or profession.

(3) "Debtor in bankruptcy" means a person who is the subject of:

    (a) An order for relief under Title 11, United States Code, or a comparable order under a successor statute of general application; or

    (b) A comparable order under federal or state law governing insolvency.

(4) "Distribution" means a transfer of money or other property from a partnership to a partner in the partner's capacity as a partner or to the partner's transferee.

(5) "Partnership" means an association of two or more persons to carry on as coowners a business for profit formed under s. 12, predecessor law, or the comparable law of another jurisdiction.

(6) "Partnership agreement" means an agreement, whether written, oral, or implied, among the partners concerning the partnership, including amendments to the partnership agreement.

(7) "Partnership at will" means a partnership in which the partners have not agreed to remain partners until the expiration of a definite term or the completion of a particular undertaking.

(8) "Partnership interest" or "partner's interest in the partnership" means all of a partner's interests in the partnership, including the partner's transferable interest and all management and other rights.

(9) "Person" means and individual, corporation, business trust, estate, trust, partnership, limited partnership, association, joint venture, limited liability company, government, governmental subdivision, agency, or instrumentality, or any other legal or commercial entity.

(10) "Property" means all property, real, personal, or mixed, tangible or intangible, or any interest therein.

(11) "Registration" or "registration statement" means a partnership registration statement filed with the Department of State under s. 7.

(12) "State" means a state of the United States, the District of Columbia, the Commonwealth of Puerto Rico, or any territory or insular possession subject to the jurisdiction of the United States.

(13) "Statement" means a statement of partnership authority under s. 17, a statement of denial under s. 45, a statement of merger under s. 54, or an amendment or cancellation of any of the foregoing.

(14) "Transfer" includes an assignment, conveyance, lease, mortgage, deed, or encumbrance.

### Section 4. Knowledge and notice.

(1) A person knows a fact if the person has actual knowledge of the fact.

(2) A person has notice of a fact if the person:
    (a) Knows the fact;
    (b) Has received a notification of the fact; or
    (c) Has reason to know the fact exists from all other facts known to the person at the time in question.

(3) A person notifies or gives a notification to another by taking steps reasonably required to inform the other person in the ordinary course, whether or not the other person learns of it.

(4) A person receives a notification when the notification:
    (a) Comes to the person's attention; or
    (b) Is duly delivered at the person's place of business or at any other place held out by the person as a place for receiving communications.

(5) Except as otherwise provided in subsection (6), a person other than an individual knows, has notice, or receives a notification of a fact for purposes of a particular transaction when the individual conducting the transaction knows, has notice, or receives a notification of the fact, or in any event when the fact would have been brought to the individual's attention if the person had exercised reasonable diligence. The person exercises reasonable diligence if the person maintains reasonable routines for communicating significant information to an individual conducting a transaction and there is reasonable compliance with the routines. Reasonable diligence does not require an individual acting for the person to communicate information unless the communication is part of the individual's regular duties or the individual has reason to know of the transaction and that the transaction would be materially affected by the information.

(6) A partner's knowledge, notice, or receipt of a notification of a fact relating to the partnership is effective immediately as knowledge by, notice to, or receipt of a notification by the partnership, except in the case of a fraud on the partnership committed by or with the consent of that partner.

### Section 5. Effect of partnership agreement; nonwaivable provisions.

(1) Except as otherwise provided in subsection (2), relations among partners and between partners and a partnership are governed by the partnership agreement. To the extent the partnership agreement does not otherwise provide, this act governs relations among partners and between partners and a partnership.

(2) The partnership agreement may not:
    (a)  1. Vary the rights and duties under s. 7 [relating to filing a registration statement] except to eliminate the duty to provide copies of statements to all of the partners.
        2. Unreasonably restrict the right of access to books and records under s. 25 (2) and (3); or
        3. Eliminate the duty of loyalty under s. 26 (2) or s. 36(2)(c), but the partnership agreement may identify specific types or categories of activities that do not violate the duty of loyalty, if not manifestly unreasonable, or all of the partners or a number or percentage specified in the partnership agreement may authorize or ratify, after full disclosure of all material facts, a specific act or transaction that otherwise would violate the duty or loyalty;
    (b) Unreasonably reduce the duty of care under s. 26 (3) or s. 35 (2)(c);
    (c) Eliminate the obligation of good faith and fair dealing under s. 26 (4), but the partnership agreement may prescribe the standards by which the performance of the obligation is to be measured if the standards are not manifestly unreasonable
    (d) Vary the power to dissociate as a partner under s. 34 (1), except to require the notice under s. 33 (1) to be in writing;
    (e) Vary the right of a court to expel a partner under the events specified in 33 (5);
    (f) Vary the requirement to wind up partnership business in cases specified in s. 33 (4), (5), or (6);
    (g) Change the notice provisions contained in s. 49 (6) or s. 52 (6); or
    (h) Restrict rights of third parties under this act.

### Section 6. Supplemental principles of law.

(1) Unless displaced by particular provisions of this act, the principles of law and equity supplement this act.

(2) If an obligation to pay interest arises under this act and the rate is not specified, the rate is that specified in s. _____ *{will refer to pertinent interest rate section of state law}.*

**Section 7.**  **Execution, filing, and recording of partnership registration and other statements.**

(1)  A partnership may file a partnership registration statement with the Department of State, which must include:

    (a)  The name of the partnership, which must be filed for purpose of public notice only and shall create no presumption of ownership beyond that which is created under the common las and which shall be recorded by the Department of State without regard to any other name recordation.

    (b)  The street address of the chief executive office of the partnership in this state, if there is one.

    (c)  1.  The names and mailing addresses of all partners of the partnership; or

        2.  The name and street address of an agent appointed and maintained by the partnership, who shall maintain a list of the names and mailing addresses of all of the partners of the partnership and, on request for good cause shown, shall make the list available to any person at an office open from at least 10 a.m. to 12 noon each day, except Saturdays, Sundays, and legal holidays.

    (d)  The partnership's federal employer identification number.

    (e)  The recorded document number of a partner or agent named pursuant to subparagraph (c)2. that is a person other than an individual.

(2)  The Department of State shall file a partnership registration statement under subsection (1) without regard to th use of the same or a similar name by another partnership registered or other entity organized or qualified in this state. The use of a partnership name in a registration statement filed with the Department of State is for the purpose of public notice only and does not create a presumption of ownership of the name used beyond that acquired under the common law.

(3)  Each partner of a registered partnership, and any agent named pursuant to subparagraph (1)(c)2. that is a legal or other commercial entity, and not an individual, must:

    (a)  Be organized or otherwise registered with the Department of State as required by law.

    (b)  Maintain an active status with the Department of State.

    (c)  Not be dissolved, revoked, canceled, or withdrawn.

(4)  Except as provided in s. 18 or s. 39, a statement may be filed with the Department of State only if the partnership has filed a registration statement pursuant to subsection (1). A certified copy of a statement that is filed in a jurisdiction other than this state may be filed with the Department of State in lieu of an original statement. Any such filing has the effect provided in this act with respect to partnership property located in, or transactions that occur in, this state.

(5)  A partnership registration statement or other statement must be delivered to the Department of State for filing, which may include electronic filing and must be typewritten or legibly printed in the English language.

(6)  A statement filed by a partnership must be executed by at least two partners. Other statements must be executed by a partner or other person authorized by this act. The execution of a statement by an individual as, or on behalf of, a partner or other person named as a partner in a filing constitutes an affirmation under the penalties of perjury that the facts state therein are true.

(7)  A partnership may amend or cancel its registration, and a person authorized by this act to file a statement may amend or cancel the statement, by filing an amendment or cancellation that:

    (a)  Identifies the partnership and the statement being amended or canceled.

    (b)  States the substance of what is being amended or canceled.

(8)  A certified copy of a statement that has been filed with the Department of State and recorded in the office for recording transfers of real property has the effect provided for

recorded statements in this act. A recorded statement that is not a certified copy of a statement filed with the Department of State does not have the effect provided for recorded statements in this act.

(9) A person who files a statement pursuant to this section shall promptly send a copy of the statement to every non-filing partner and to any other person named as a partner in the statement. Failure to send a copy of a statement to a partner or other person does not limit the effectiveness of the statement as to a person who is not a partner.

(10) If a document is determined by the Department of State to be incomplete and inappropriate for filing, the Department of State shall return the document to the person or entity filing it within 15 days after the document was received for filing, together with a brief written explanation of the reason for the refusal to file the document. If the applicant returns the document with corrections in accordance with the rules of the Department of State within 60 days after it was mailed to the applicant by the Department of State and, if at the time of return the applicant so requests in writing, the filing date of the document will be the filing date that would have been applied had the original document not been deficient, except as to persons who relied on the record before correction and were adversely affected thereby.

### Section 8. Fees for filing documents and issuing certificates; powers of the Department of State.

(1) The Department of State shall collect the following fees when documents authorized by this act are delivered to the Department of State for filing:
- (a) Partnership registration statement: $__.
- (b) Statement of partnership authority: $__.
- (c) Statement of denial: $__.
- (d) Statement of dissociation: $__.
- (e) Statement of dissolution: $__.
- (f) Statement of merger for each party thereto: $__.
- (g) Amendment to any statement or registration: $__.
- (h) Cancellation of any statement or registration: $__.
- (i) Certified copy of any recording or part thereof: $__.
- (j) Certificate of status: $__.
- (k) Any other document required or permitted to be filed by this act: $__.

(2) The Department of State has the power and authority reasonably necessary to enable it to administer this act efficiently, to perform the duties imposed upon it by this act, and to adopt reasonable rules necessary to carry out its duties and functions under this act.

### Section 9. Law governing internal relations.

The law of the jurisdiction in which a partnership has its chief executive office governs relations among partners and between the partners and a partnership.

### Section 10. Partnership subject to amendment or repeal of act.

A partnership governed by this act is subject to any amendment to or repeal of this act.

### Section 11. Partnership as entity.

A partnership is an entity distinct from its partners.

### Section 12. Formation of partnership.

(1) Except as otherwise provided in subsection (2), the association of two or more persons to carry on as coowners a business for profit forms a partnership, whether or not the persons intend to form a partnership.

(2) An association formed under a statute, other than this act, a predecessor statute, or a comparable law of another jurisdiction is not a partnership under this act.

(3) In determining whether a partnership is formed, the following rules apply:
- (a) Joint tenancy, tenancy in common, tenancy by the entireties, joint property, common property, or part ownership does not, by itself, establish a partnership, even if the coowners share profits made by the use of the property.
- (b) The sharing of gross returns does not, by itself, establish a partnership, even if the persons sharing them have a joint or common right or interest in property from which the returns are derived.

(c) A person who receives a share of the profits of a business is presumed to be a partner in the business, unless the profits were received in payment:

1. Of a debt by installments or otherwise;
2. For services as an independent contractor or of wages or other compensation of an employee;
3. Of rent;
4. Of an annuity or other retirement benefit to a beneficiary, representative, or designee of a deceased or retired partner;
5. Of interest or other charge on a loan, even if the amount of payment varies with the profits of the business, including a direct or indirect present or future ownership of the collateral, or rights to income, proceeds, or increase in value derived from the collateral; or
6. For the sale of the goodwill of a business or other property by installments or otherwise.

### Section 13. Partnership property.

Property acquired by a partnership is property of the partnership and not of the partners individually.

### Section 14. When property is partnership property.

(1) Property is partnership property if acquired in the name of:
 (a) The partnership; or
 (b) One or more partners with an indication in the instrument transferring title to the property of the person's capacity as a partner or of the existence of a partnership but without an indication of the name of the partnership.
(2) Property is acquired in the name of the partnership by a transfer to:
 (a) The partnership in its name; or
 (b) One or more partners in their capacity as partners in the partnership, if the name of the partnership is indicated in the instrument transferring title to the property.
(3) Property is presumed to be partnership property if purchased with partnership assets, even if not acquired in the name of the partnership or one or more partners with an indication in the instrument transferring title to the property of the person's capacity as a partner or of the existence of a partnership.
(4) Property acquired in the name of one or more of the partners, without an indication in the instrument transferring title to the property of the person's capacity as a partner or of the existence of a partnership and without use of partnership assets, is presumed to be separate property, even if used for partnership purposes.

### Section 15. Partner agent of partnership.

Subject to the effect of a statement of partnership authority under s. 17:

(1) Each partner is an agent of the partnership for the purpose of its business. An act of a partner, including the execution of an instrument in the partnership name, for apparently carrying on in the ordinary course of partnership business or business of the kind carried on by the partnership, in the geographic area in which the partnership operates, binds the partnership unless the partner had no authority to act for the partnership in the particular matter and the person with whom the partner was dealing knew or had received notification that the partner lacked authority.
(2) An act of a partner which is not apparently for carrying in the ordinary course of the partnership business or business of the kind carried on by the partnership binds the partnership only if the act was authorized by all of the other partners or is authorized by the terms of a written partnership agreement.

### Section 16. Transfer of partnership property.

(1) Partnership property may be transferred as follows:
 (a) Subject to the effect of a statement of partnership authority under s. 17, partnership property held in the name of the partnership may be transferred by an instrument of transfer executed by a partner in the partnership name.
 (b) Partnership property held in the name of one or more partners with an indication in the instrument transferring the property to them of their capacity as partners or of the existence of a partnership, but without an indication of the name of the partnership, may be transferred by an instrument of transfer executed by the persons in whose name the property is held.

(c) Partnership property held in the name of one or more persons other than the partnership, without an indication in the instrument transferring the property to them of their capacity as partners or of the existence of a partnership, may be transferred by an instrument of transfer executed by the persons in whose name the property is held.

(2) A partnership may recover partnership property from a transferee only if the partnership proves that execution of the instrument of initial transfer did not bind the partnership under s. 15 and:

(a) As to a subsequent transferee who gave value for property transferred under paragraph (1)(a) or paragraph (1)(b), proves that the subsequent transferee knew or had received a notification that the person who executed the instrument of initial transfer lacked authority to bind the partnership; or

(b) As to a transferee who gave value for property transferred under paragraph (1)(c), proves that the transferee knew or had received a notification that the property was partnership property and that the person who executed the instrument of initial transfer lacked authority to bind the partnership.

(3) A partnership may not recover partnership property from a subsequent transferee if the partnership would not have been entitled to recover the property under subsection (2) from any earlier transferee of the property.

(4) If a person holds all of the partners' interests in the partnership, all of the partnership property vests in such person. Such person may execute a document in the name of the partnership to evidence vesting of the property in such person and may file or record the document.

## Section 17.  Statement of partnership authority.

(1) A partnership may file a statement of partnership authority, which:

(a) Must include the name of the partnership, as identified in the records of the Department of State, and the names of the partners authorized to execute an instrument transferring real property held in the name of the partnership.

(b) May also state or include the authority, or limitations on the authority, of some or all of the partners to enter into other transactions on behalf of the partnership, and any other matter.

(2) If a filed statement of partnership authority is executed pursuant to s. 7 (3) and states the name of the partnership but does not contain all of the other information required by subsection (1), the statement nevertheless operates with respect to a person not a partner as provided in subsections (3) and (4).

(3) Except as provided in subsection (6), a filed statement of partnership authority supplements the authority of a partner to enter into transactions on behalf of the partnership as follows:

(a) Except for transfers of real property, a grant of authority contained in a filed statement of partnership authority is conclusive in favor of a person who gives value without knowledge to the contrary, so long as and to the extent that a limitation on that authority is not then contained in another filed statement. A filed cancellation of a limitation on authority revives the previous grant of authority.

(b) A grant of authority to transfer real property held in the name of the partnership contained in a certified copy of a filed statement of partnership authority recorded in the office for recording transfers of such real property is conclusive in favor of a person who gives value without knowledge to the contrary, so long as and to the extent that a certified copy of a filed statement containing a limitation on such authority is not then of record in the office for recording transfers of such real property. The recording in the office for recording transfers of such real property of a certified copy of a filed cancellation of a limitation on authority revives the previous grant of authority.

(4) A person who is not a partner is deemed to know of a limitation on the authority of a partner to transfer real property held in the name of the partnership if a certified copy of the filed statement containing the limitation on authority is of record in the office for recording transfers of such real property.

(5) Except as otherwise provided in subsections (3) and (4) and ss. 39 and 45, a person not a partner is not deemed to know of a limitation on the authority of a partner merely because the limitation is contained in a filed statement.

(6) Unless earlier canceled, a filed statement of partnership authority is canceled by operation of law 5 years after the date on which the statement, or the most recent amendment, was filed with the Department of State.

## Section 18.  Statement of denial.

(1) A partner or other person named as a partner in a filed registration, statement of partnership authority, or in a list maintained by an agent pursuant to s. 7 (1)(c) may file a statement of denial stating:

(a) The name of the partnership, as identified in the records of the Department of State; and

(b) The fact that is being denied, which may include denial of a person's authority or status as a partner.

(2) A statement of denial may be filed without regard to the provisions of s. 7 (4) if it states that no partnership registration statement has been filed with the Department of State.

(3) A statement of denial is a limitation on authority as provided in s. 17 (5) and (6).

### Section 19.  Partnership liable for partner's actionable conduct.

(1) A partnership is liable for loss or injury caused to a person, or for a penalty incurred, as a result of a wrongful act or omission, or other actionable conduct, of a partner acting in the ordinary course of business of the partnership or with authority of the partnership.

(2) If, in the course of the partnership's business or while acting with authority of the partnership, a partner receives or causes the partnership to receive money or property of a person who is not a partner, and the money or property is misapplied by a partner, the partnership is liable for the loss.

### Section 20.  Partner's liability.

(1) Except as otherwise provided in subsection (2), all partners are liable jointly and severally for all obligations of the partnership unless otherwise agreed by a claimant or provided by law.

(2) A person admitted as a partner into an existing partnership is not personally liable for any partnership obligation incurred before the person's admission as a partner.

### Section 21.  Actions by and against partnership and partners.

(1) A partnership may sue and be sued in the name of the partnership.

(2) An action may be brought against the partnership and any or all of the partners in the same action or in separate actions.

(3) A judgment against a partnership is not by itself a judgment against a partner. A judgment against a partnership may not be satisfied from a partner's assets unless there is also a judgment against the partner.

(4) A judgment creditor of a partner may perfect a judgment lien but may not proceed against or otherwise levy or execute against the assets of the partner to satisfy a judgment arising from a partnership obligation or liability unless:

    (a) A judgment based on the same claim has been obtained against the partnership and a writ of execution on the judgment has been returned unsatisfied in whole or in part;

    (b) The partnership is a debtor in bankruptcy;

    (c) The partner has agreed that the creditor need not exhaust partnership assets;

    (d) A court grants permission to the judgment creditor to proceed against or otherwise levy or execute against the assets of a partner based on a finding that partnership assets subject to execution are clearly insufficient to satisfy the judgment, that exhaustion of partnership assets is excessively burdensome, or that the grant of permission is an appropriate exercise of the court's equitable powers; or

    (e) Liability is imposed on the partner by law or contract independent of the existence of the partnership.

(5) This section applies to any partnership liability or obligation resulting from a representation by a partner or purported partner under s. 22.

### Section 22.  Liability of purported partner.

(1) If a person, by words or conduct, represents himself, purports to be a partner, or consents to being represented by another as a partner, in a partnership or with one or more persons who are not partners, the purported partner is liable to a person to whom the representation is made if such person, relying on the representation, enters into a transaction with the actual or purported partnership. If the representation, either by the purported partner or by a person with the purported partner's consent, is made in a public manner, the purported partner is liable to a person who relies upon the purported partnership even if the purported partner is not aware of being held out as a partner to the claimant. If partnership liability results, the purported partner is liable with respect to such liability as if the purported partner were a partner. If no partnership liability results, the purported partner is liable with respect to such liability jointly and severally with any other person consenting to the representation.

(2) If a person is thus represented to be partner in an existing partnership, or with one or more persons who are not partners, the purported partner is an agent of persons consenting to the representation to bind them to the same extent and in the same manner as if the purported partner were a partner, with respect to persons who entered into transactions in reliance upon the representation. If all of the partners of the existing partnership consent to

the representation, a partnership act or obligation results. If fewer than all of the partners of the existing partnership consent to the representation, the person acting and the partners consenting to the representation are jointly and severally liable.

(3) A person is not liable as a partner merely because the person is named by another in a statement of partnership authority.

(4) A person does not continue to be liable as a partner merely because of a failure to file a statement of dissociation or to amend a statement of partnership authority to indicate the partner's dissociation from the partnership.

(5) Except as otherwise provided in subsection (1) and (2), persons who are not partners as to each other are not liable as partners to other persons.

## Section 23.    Partner's rights and duties.

(1) Each partner is deemed to have an account which is:

    (a) Credited with an amount equal to the money plus the value of any of the property, net of the amount or any liabilities, the partner contributes to the partnership and the partner's share of the partnership profits; and

    (b) Charged with an amount equal to the money plus the value of any other property, net of the amount of any liabilities, distributed by the partnership to the partner and the partner's share of the partnership losses.

(2) Each partner is entitled to an equal share of the partnership profits and is chargeable with a share of the partnership losses in proportion to the partner's share of the profits.

(3) A partnership shall reimburse a partner for payments made and indemnify a partner for liabilities incurred by the partner in the ordinary course of the business of the partnership or for the preservation of its business or property.

(4) A partnership shall reimburse a partner for an advance to the partnership beyond the amount of capital the partner agreed to contribute.

(5) A payment or advance made by a partner which gives rise to a partnership obligation under subsection (3) or subsection (4) constitutes a loan to the partnership which accrues interest from the date of the payment or advance.

(6) Each partner has equal rights in the management and conduct of the partnership business.

(7) A partner may use or possess partnership property only on behalf of the partnership.

(8) A partner is not entitled to remuneration for services performed for the partnership, except for reasonable compensation for services rendered in winding up the business of the partnership.

(9) A person may become a partner only with the consent of all of the partners.

(10) A difference arising as to a matter in the ordinary course of business of a partnership my be decided by a majority of the partners. An act outside the ordinary course of business of a partnership and an amendment to the partnership agreement may be undertaken only with the consent of all of the partners.

(11) This section does not affect the obligations of a partnership to other persons under s. 15.

## Section 24.    Distribution in kind.

A partner has no right to receive, and may not be required to accept, a distribution in kind.

## Section 25.    Partner's rights and duties with respect to information.

(1) A partnership shall keep its books and records, if any, at the chief executive office of the partnership.

(2) A partnership shall provide partners and their agents and attorneys access to the books and records of the partnership. The partnership shall provide former partners and their agents and attorneys access to books and records pertaining to the period during with they were partners. The right of access provides the opportunity to inspect and copy books and records during ordinary business hours. A partnership may impose a reasonable charge, covering the costs of labor and material, for copies of documents furnished.

(3) Each partner and the partnership shall furnish to a partner, and to the legal representative of a deceased partner or partner under legal disability:

    (a) Without demand, any information concerning the partnership's business and affairs reasonably required for the proper exercise of the partner's rights and duties under the partnership agreement or this act; and

    (b) Upon demand, any other information concerning the partnership's business and affairs, except to the extent the demand or the information demanded is unreasonable or otherwise improper under the circumstances.

**Section 26.    General standards of partner's conduct.**

(1)   The only fiduciary duties a partner owes to the partnership and the other partners are the duty of loyalty and the duty of care, as set forth in subsections (2) and (3).

(2)   A partner's duty of loyalty to the partnership and the other partners includes, without limitation, the following:

   (a)   To account to the partnership and hold as trustee for the partnership any property, profit, or benefit derived by the partner in the conduct and winding up of the partnership business or derived from a use by the partner of partnership property, including the appropriation of a partnership opportunity;

   (b)   To refrain from dealing with the partnership in the conduct or winding up of the partnership business as or on behalf of a party having an interest adverse to the partnership; and

   (c)   To refrain from competing with the partnership in the conduct or the partnership business before the dissolution of the partnership.

(3)   A partner's duty of care to the partnership and the other partners in the conduct and winding up of the partnership business is limited to refraining from engaging in grossly negligent or reckless conduct, intentional misconduct, or a knowing violation of the law.

(4)   A partner shall discharge the duties to the partnership and the other partners under this act or under the partnership agreement and exercise any rights consistently with the obligation of good faith and fair dealing.

(5)   A partner does not violate a duty or obligation under this act or under a partnership agreement merely because the partner's conduct furthers the partner's own interest.

(6)   A partner may lend money to and transact other business with the partnership, and as to each loan or transaction, the rights and obligations of the partner are the same as those of a person who is not a partner, subject to other applicable law.

(7)   This section applies to a person winding up the partnership business as the personal or legal representative of the last surviving partner as if the person were a partner.

**Section 27.    Actions by partnership and partners.**

(1)   A partnership may maintain an action against a partner for a breach of the partnership agreement, or for the violation of a duty to the partnership, causing harm to the partnership.

(2)   A partner may maintain an action against the partnership or another partner for legal or equitable relief, with or without an accounting as to partnership business, to:

   (a)   Enforce such partner's rights under the partnership agreement;

   (b)   Enforce such partner's rights under this act, including:

      1.   Such partner's rights under s. 23, s. 25, or s. 26;

      2.   Such partner's right upon dissociation to have the partner's interest in the partnership purchased pursuant to s. 36 or enforce any other right under ss. 33 - 40; or

      3.   Such partner's right to compel a dissolution and winding up of the partnership business under s. 620.8801 or enforce any other right under ss. 41 - 47; or

   (c)   Enforce the rights and otherwise protect the interests of such partner, including rights and interests arising independently of the partnership relationship.

(3)   The accrual of, and any time limitation on, a right of action for a remedy under this section is governed by other law. A right to an accounting upon a dissolution and winding up does not revive a claim barred by law.

**Section 28.    Continuation of partnership beyond definite term or particular undertaking.**

(1)   When a partnership for a fixed term or particular undertaking is continued after the termination of the term or undertaking without an express agreement, the rights and duties of the partners remain the same as they were at termination so far as is consistent with a partnership at will.

(2)   A continuation of the business by the partners or such of them as habitually acted in it during the term without any settlement or liquidation of the partnership affairs is prima facie evidence of a continuation of the partnership.

**Section 29.    Partner not coowner of partnership property.**

Partnership property is owned by the partnership as an entity, not by the partners as coowners. A partner has no interest that can be transferred, either voluntarily or involuntarily, in specific partnership property.

**Section 30.    Partner's transferable interest in partnership.**
The only transferable interest of a partner in the partnership is the partner's share of the profits and losses of the partnership and the partner's right to receive distributions. A partner's interest in the partnership is personal property.

**Section 31.    Transfer of partner's transferable interest.**
(1)  A transfer, in whole or in part, of a partner's transferable interest in the partnership:
    (a)  Is permissible.
    (b)  Does not, by itself, cause the partner's dissociation or a dissolution and winding up of the partnership business.
    (c)  Does not, as against the other partners or the partnership, entitle the transferee, during the continuance of the partnership, to participate in the management or conduct of the partnership business, to require access to information concerning partnership transactions, or to inspect or copy the partnership books or records.
(2)  A transferee of a partner's transferable interest in the partnership has a right:
    (a)  To receive, in accordance with the transfer, distributions to which the transferor would otherwise be entitled;
    (b)  To receive upon the dissolution and winding up of the partnership business, in accordance with the transfer, the net amount otherwise distributable to the transferor; and
    (c)  To seek a judicial determination that it is equitable to wind up the partnership business.
(3)  In a dissolution and winding up of a partnership, a transferee is entitled to an account of partnership transactions only from the date of the latest account agreed to by all the partners.
(4)  Upon transfer, the transfer or retains the rights and duties of a partner other than the interest in distributions transferred.
(5)  A partnership need not give effect to a transferee's rights under this section until it has notice of the transfer.
(6)  A transfer of a partner's transferable interest in the partnership in violation of a restriction on transfer contained in the partnership agreement is ineffective as to a person having notice of the restriction at the time of transfer.

**Section 32.    Partner's transferable interest subject to charging order.**
(1)  Upon application by a judgment creditor of a partner or of a partner's transferee, a court having jurisdiction may charge the transferable interest of the judgment debtor to satisfy the judgment. The court may appoint a receiver of the share of the distributions due or to become due to the judgment debtor in respect of the partnership and make all other orders, directions, accounts, and inquiries the judgment debtor might have made or which the circumstances of the case may require.
(2)  A charging order constitutes a lien on the judgment debtor's transferable interest in the partnership. The court may order a foreclosure on the interest subject to the charging order at any time. The purchaser at the foreclosure sale has the rights of a transferee.
(3)  At any time before foreclosure, an interest charged may be redeemed:
    (a)  By the judgment debtor;
    (b)  With property other than partnership property, by one or more of the other partners; or
    (c)  With partnership property, by any one or more of the other partners with the consent of all of the partners whose interests are not so charged.
(4)  This act does not deprive a partner of a right under exemption laws with respect to the partner's interest in the partnership.
(5)  This section provides the exclusive remedy by which a judgment creditor or a partner or partner's transferee may satisfy a judgment out of the judgment debtor's transferable interest in the partnership.

**Section 33.    Events causing partner's dissociation.**
A partner is dissociated from a partnership upon the occurrence of any of the following events:
(1)  The partnership having notice of the partner's express will to immediately withdraw as a partner or withdraw on a later date specified by the partner;
(2)  An event agreed to in the partnership agreement causing the partner's dissociation;
(3)  The partner's expulsion pursuant to the partnership agreement;
(4)  The partner's expulsion by a unanimous vote of the other partners if:
    (a)  It is unlawful to carry on the partnership business with such partner;

(b)	There has been a transfer of all or substantially all of such partner's transferable interest in the partnership other than a transfer for security purposes, or a court order charging the partner's interest, which has not been foreclosed;

(c)	Within 90 days after the partnership notifies a corporate partner that it will be expelled because it has filed a certificate of dissolution or the equivalent, its charter has been revoked, or its right to conduct business has been suspended by the jurisdiction of its incorporation, there is no revocation of the certificate of dissolution or no reinstatement of the corporate partner's charter or the corporate partner's right to conduct business; or

(d)	A partnership that is a partner has been dissolved and its business is being wound up;

(5)	On application by the partnership or another partner, the partner's expulsion by judicial determination because:

   (a)	The partner engaged in wrongful conduct that adversely and materially affected the partnership business;

   (b)	The partner willfully or persistently committed a material breach of the partnership agreement or of a duty owed to the partnership or the other partners under s. 26; or

   (c)	The partner engaged in conduct relating to the partnership business which makes it not reasonably practicable to carry on the business in partnership with the partner;

(6)	The partner's:

   (a)	Becoming a debtor in bankruptcy;

   (b)	Executing an assignment for the benefit of creditors;

   (c)	Seeking, consenting to, or acquiescing in the appointment of a trustee, receiver, or liquidator of such partner or of all or substantially all of such partner's property; or

   (d)	Failing, within 90 days after appointment, to have vacated or have stayed the appointment of a trustee, receiver, or liquidator of the partner or of all or substantially all of the partner's property obtained without the partner's consent or acquiescence, or failing within 90 days after the expiration of a stay to have the appointment vacated;

(7)	In the case of a partner who is an individual:

   (a)	The partner's death;

   (b)	The appointment of a guardian or general conservator for the partner; or

   (c)	A judicial determination that the partner has otherwise become incapable of performing the partner's duties under the partnership agreement;

(8)	In the case of a partner that is a trust or is acting as a partner by virtue of being a trustee of a trust, distribution of the trust's entire transferable interest in the partnership, but not merely by reason of the substitution of a successor trustee;

(9)	In the case of a partner that is an estate or is acting as a partner by virtue of being a personal representative of an estate, distribution of the estate's entire transferable interest in the partnership, but not merely by reason of the substitution of a successor personal representative; or

(10)	Termination of a partner who is not an individual, partnership, corporation, trust, or estate.

### Section 34.	Partner's power to dissociate; wrongful dissociation.

(1)	A partner has the power to dissociate at any time, rightfully or wrongfully, by express will pursuant to s. 33 (1).

(2)	A partner's dissociation is wrongful only if:

   (a)	It is in breach of an express provision of the partnership agreement; or

   (b)	In the case of a partnership for a definite term or particular undertaking, before the expiration of the term or the completion of the undertaking:

      1.	The partner withdraws by express will, unless the withdrawal follows within 90 days after another partner's dissociation by death, or otherwise under s. 33 (6)-(10) or wrongful dissociation under this subsection;

      2.	The partner is expelled by judicial determination under s. 33 (5);

      3.	The partner is dissociated by becoming a debtor in bankruptcy; or

      4.	In the case of a partner who is not an individual, trust other than a business trust, or estate, the partner is expelled or otherwise dissociated because the partner willfully dissolved or terminated.

(3)	A partner who wrongfully dissociates is liable to the partnership and to the other partners for damages caused by the dissociation. The liability is in addition to any other obligation of the partner to the partnership or to the other partners.

**Section 35.    Effect of partner's dissociation.**

(1)  If a partner's dissociation results in a dissolution and winding up of the partnership business, ss. 41-47 apply; otherwise, ss. 36-40 apply.

(2)  Upon a partner's dissociation:

    (a)  The partner's right to participate in the management and conduct of the partnership business terminates, except as otherwise provided in s. 43;

    (b)  The partner's duty of loyalty under s. 26 (2)(c) terminates; and

    (c)  The partner's duty of loyalty under s. 26 (2)(a) and (b) and duty of care under s. 26 (3) continue only with regard to matters arising and events occurring before the partner's dissociation, unless the partner participates in winding up the partnership's business pursuant to s. 43.

**Section 36.    Purchase of dissociated partner's interest.**

(1)  If a partner is dissociated from a partnership without resulting in a dissolution and winding up of the partnership business under s. 41, the partnership shall cause the dissociated partner's interest in the partnership to be purchased for a buyout price determined pursuant to subsection (2).

(2)  The buyout price of a dissociated partner's interest is the amount that would have been distributed to the dissociating partner under s. 47 (2) if, on the date of dissociation, the assets of the partnership were sold at a price equal to the greater of the liquidation value of the assets or the value of the assets based upon a sale of the entire business as a going concern without having the dissociated partner and the partnership wind up as of such date. Interest must be paid from the date of dissociation to the date of payment.

(3)  Damages for wrongful dissociation under s. 34 (2), and all other amounts owning, whether or not presently due, from the dissociated partner to the partnership, must be offset against the buyout price. Interest must be paid from the date the amount owed becomes due to the date of payment.

(4)  A partnership shall indemnify a dissociated partner whose interest is being purchased against all partnership liabilities, whether incurred before or after the dissociation, except liabilities incurred by an act of the dissociated partner under s. 37.

(5)  If no agreement for the purchase of a dissociated partner's interest is reached within 120 days after a written demand for payment, the partnership shall pay, or cause to be paid, in cash to the dissociated partner the amount the partnership estimates to be the buyout price and accrued interest, reduced by any offsets and accrued interest under subsection (3).

(6)  If a deferred payment is authorized under subsection (8), the partnership may tender a written offer to pay the amount it estimates to be the buyout price and accrued interest, reduced by any offsets under subsection (3), stating the time of payment, the amount and type of security for payment, and the other terms and conditions of the obligation.

(7)  The payment or tender required by subsection (5) or subsection (6) must be accompanied by the following:

    (a)  A statement of partnership assets and liabilities as of the date of dissociation;

    (b)  The latest available partnership balance sheet and income statement, if any;

    (c)  An explanation of how the estimated amount of the payment was calculated; and

    (d)  Written notice that the payment is in full satisfaction of the obligation to purchase unless, within 120 days after the written notice, the dissociated partner commences an action to determine the buyout price, any offsets under subsection (3), or other terms of the obligation to purchase.

(8)  A partner who wrongfully dissociates before the expiration of a definite term or the completion of a particular undertaking is not entitled to payment of any portion of the buyout price until the expiration of the term or completion of the undertaking, unless the partner establishes to the satisfaction of the court that earlier payment will not cause undue hardship to the business of the partnership. A deferred payment must be adequately secured and shall bear interest.

(9)  A dissociated partner may maintain an action against the partnership, pursuant to s. 27 (2)(b)2., to determine the buyout price of that partner's interest, any offsets under subsection (3), or other terms of the obligation to purchase. The action must be commenced within 120 days after the partnership has tendered payment or an offer to pay or within 1 year after written demand for payment if no payment or offer to pay is tendered. The court shall determine the buyout price of the dissociated partner's interest, any offset due under subsection (3), and accrued interest, and enter judgment for any additional payment or refund. If deferred payment is authorized under subsection (8), the court shall also determine the security for payment and other terms of the obligation to purchase. The court may assess reasonable attorney's fees and the fees and expenses of appraisers or other experts for a party

to the action, in amounts the court finds equitable, against a party that the court finds acted arbitrarily, vexatiously, or not in good faith. The finding may be based on the partnership's failure to tender payment or an offer to pay or to comply with subsection (7).

**Section 37.    Dissociated partner's power to bind and liability to partnership.**
   (1)  For 1 year after a partner dissociates without resulting in a dissolution and winding up of the partnership business, the partnership, including a surviving partnership under ss. 48 - 55, is bound by an act of the dissociated partner which would have bound the partnership under s. 15 before dissociation only if, at the time of entering into the transaction, the other party:
      (a)  Reasonably believed that the dissociated partner was then a partner;
      (b)  Did not have notice of the partner's dissociation; and
      (c)  Is not deemed to have had knowledge under s. 17 (5) or notice under s. 39 (4).
   (2)  A dissociated partner is liable to the partnership for any damage caused to the partnership arising from an obligation incurred by the dissociated partner after dissociation for which the partnership is liable under subsection (1).

**Section 38.    Dissociated partner's liability to other persons.**
   (1)  A partner's dissociation does not, by itself, discharge the partner's liability for a partnership obligation incurred before dissociation. A dissociated partner is not liable for a partnership obligation incurred after dissociation, except as otherwise provided in subsection (2).
   (2)  A partner who dissociates without resulting in a dissolution and winding up of the partnership business is liable as a partner to any other party to a transaction entered into by the partnership, or a surviving partnership under ss. 48 - 55, within 1 year after the partner's dissociation only if, at the time of entering into the transaction, the other party:
      (a)  Reasonably believed that the dissociated partner was then a partner;
      (b)  Did not have notice of the partner's dissociation; and
      (c)  Is not deemed to have had knowledge under s. 19 3(5).
   (3)  By agreement with the partnership creditor and the partners continuing the business, a dissociated partner may be released from liability for a partnership obligation.
   (4)  A dissociated partner is released from liability for a partnership obligation if a partnership creditor, with notice of the partner's dissociation but without the partner's consent, agrees to a material alteration in the nature or time of payment of a partnership obligation.

**Section 39.    Statement of dissociation.**
   (1)  A dissociated partner or the partnership may file a statement of dissociation stating:
      (a)  The name of the partnership as identified in the records of the Department of State.
      (b)  That the partner is dissociated from the partnership.
   (2)  A statement of dissociation may be filed without regard to the provisions of s. 7 (4) if it states that no partnership registration has been filed with the Department of State.
   (3)  A statement of dissociation is a limitation on the authority of a dissociated partner for purposes of s. 18 (5) and (6).
   (4)  For purposes of ss. 37 (1)(c) and 38 (2)(c), a person who is not a partner is deemed to have notice of the dissociation 90 days after a statement of dissociation is filed.

**Section 40.    Continued use of partnership name.**
   Continued use of a partnership name, or a dissociated partner's name as part thereof, by partners continuing the business does not, by itself, make the dissociated partner liable for an obligation of the partners or the partnership continuing the business.

**Section 41.    Events causing dissolution and winding up of partnership business.**
   A partnership is dissolved, and its business must be wound up, only upon the occurrence of any of the following events:
   (1)  In a partnership at will, the partnership's having notice from a partner, other than a partner who is dissociated under s. 33 (2)-(10), of such partner's express will to withdraw as a partner, or withdraw on a later date specified by the partner;

(2) In a partnership for a definite term or particular undertaking:

    (a) The expiration of 90 days after a partner's dissociation by death or otherwise under s. 33 (6)-(10) or by wrongful dissociation under s. 34 (2), unless before that time a majority in interest of the remaining partners, including partners who have rightfully dissociated pursuant to s. 34 (2)(b)1., agree to continue the partnership;

    (b) The express will of all of the partners to wind up the partnership's business; or

    (c) The expiration of the term or the completion of the undertaking;

(3) An event agreed to in the partnership agreement resulting in the winding up of the partnership business;

(4) An event which makes it unlawful for all or substantially all of the business of the partnership to be continued, provided, a cure of the illegality, within 90 days after notice to the partnership of the event, is effective retroactive to the date of the event for purposes of this section;

(5) On application by a partner, a judicial determination that:

    (a) The economic purpose of the partnership is likely to be unreasonably frustrated;

    (b) Another partner has engaged in conduct relating to the partnership business which makes it not reasonably practicable to carry on the business in partnership with such partner; or

    (c) It is not otherwise reasonably practicable to carry on the partnership business in conformity with the partnership agreement; or

(6) On application by a transferee of a partner's transferable interest, a judicial determination that it is equitable to wind up the partnership business:

    (a) After the expiration of the term or completion of the undertaking, if the partnership was for a definite term or particular undertaking at the time of the transfer or entry of the charging order that gave rise to the transfer; or

    (b) At any time, if the partnership was a partnership at will at the time of the transfer or entry of the charging order that gave rise to the transfer.

### Section 42.    Partnership continues after dissolution.

(1) Subject to subsection (2), a partnership continues after dissolution only for the purpose of winding up its business. The partnership is terminated when the winding up of its business is completed.

(2) At any time after the dissolution of a partnership before the winding up of partnership business is completed, all of the partners, including any dissociating partner other than a wrongfully dissociating partner, may waive the right to have the partnership's business wound up and the partnership terminated. In that event:

    (a) The partnership resumes carrying on its business as if dissolution had never occurred, and any liability incurred by the partnership or a partner after the dissolution and before the waiver is determined is as if the dissolution had never occurred; and

    (b) The rights of a third party accruing under s. 44 (1) or arising out of conduct in reliance on the dissolution before the third party knew or received a notification of the waiver may not be adversely affected.

### Section 43.    Right to wind up partnership business.

(1) After dissolution, a partner who has not wrongfully dissociated may participate in winding up the partnership's business, but, upon application of any partner, partner's legal representative, or transferee, the circuit court, for good cause shown, may order judicial supervision of the winding up.

(2) The legal representative of th last surviving partner may wind up a partnership's business.

(3) A person winding up a partnership's business may preserve the partnership business or property as a going concern for a reasonable time, prosecute and defend actions and proceedings, whether civil, criminal, or administrative, settle and close the partnership's business, dispose of and transfer the partnership's property, discharge the partnership's liabilities, distribute the assets of the partnership pursuant to s. 620.8807, settle disputes by mediation or arbitration and perform any other necessary acts.

### Section 44.    Partner's power to bind partnership after dissolution.

Subject to s. 620.8805, a partnership is bound by a partner's act after dissolution which:

(1) Is appropriate for winding up the partnership business; or

(2) Would have bound the partnership under s. 15 before dissolution if any other party to the transaction did not have notice of the dissolution.

**Section 45.    Statement of dissolution.**
(1) After dissolution, a partner who has not wrongfully dissociated may file a statement of dissolution stating:
    (a) The name of the partnership, as identified in the records of the Department of State; and
    (b) That the partnership has dissolved and is winding up its business.
(2) A statement of dissolution cancels a filed statement of partnership authority for purposes of s. 620.8305(5) and is a limitation on authority for purposes of s. 17 (6).
(3) For purposes of ss. 15 and 44, a person who is not a partner is deemed to have notice of a dissolution, and the limitation on the partners' authority as a result of the statement of dissolution, 90 days after it is filed.
(4) After filing and, if appropriate, recording a statement of dissolution, a dissolved partnership may file and, if appropriate, record a statement of partnership authority which will operate with respect to a person who is not a partner, as provided in s. 17 (5) and (6), in any transaction, whether or not the transaction is appropriate for winding up the partnership business.

**Section 46.    Partner's liability to other partners after dissolution.**
(1) Except as otherwise provided in subsection (2), after dissolution, a partner is liable to the other partners for the partner's share of any partnership liability incurred under s. 44.
(2) A partner who, with knowledge of the dissolution, incurs a partnership liability under s. 44 (2) by an act that is not appropriate for winding up the partnership business is liable to the partnership for any damage caused to the partnership arising from the liability.

**Section 47.    Settlement of accounts and contributions among partners.**
(1) In winding up a partnership's business, the assets of the partnership, including the contributions of the partners required by this section, must be applied to discharge the partnership's obligations to creditors, including, to the extent permitted by law, partners who are creditors. Any surplus must be applied to pay in cash the net amount distributable to partners in accordance with their right to distributions under subsection (2).
(2) Each partner is entitled to a settlement of all partnership accounts upon winding up the partnership business. In settling accounts among the partners, any profits and losses which result from the liquidation of the partnership assets must be credited and charged to the partner's accounts. The partnership shall make a distribution to a partner in an amount equal to any excess of the credits over the charges in th partner's account. A partner shall contribute to the partnership an amount equal to any excess of the charges over the credits in the partner's account.
(3) If a partner fails to contribute, all other partners shall contribute, in the proportions in which such partners share partnership losses, the additional amount necessary to satisfy the partnership obligations. A partner or partner's legal representative may recover from the other partners any contributions the partner makes to the extent the amount contributed exceeds such partner's share.
(4) After settlement of accounts, each partner shall contribute, in the proportion in which the partner shares partnership losses, the amount necessary to satisfy partnership obligations that were not known at the time of settlement.
(5) The estate of a deceased partner is liable for such partner's obligation to contribute to the partnership.
(6) An assignee for the benefit of creditors of a partnership or a partner, or a person appointed by a court to represent creditors of a partnership or a partner, may enforce a partner's obligation to contribute to the partnership.

**Section 48.    Definitions.**
For purposes of ss. 48 — 55:
(1) "General partner" means a partner in a partnership and a general partner in a limited partnership.
(2) "Limited partner" means a limited partner in a limited partnership.
(3) "Limited partnership" means a limited partnership created under the Florida Revised Uniform Limited Partnership Act, as amended, predecessor law, or the comparable law of any other jurisdiction.
(4) "Partner" includes both a general partner and a limited partner.

**Section 49.    Conversion of partnership to limited partnership.**
*[text omitted]*

**Section 50.    Conversion of limited partnership to partnership.**
(1)  A limited partnership may be converted to a partnership pursuant to this section.
(2)  Notwithstanding any provision in a limited partnership agreement, the terms and conditions of a conversion of a limited partnership to a partnership must be approved by all of the partners.
(3)  After the conversion is approved by the partners, the limited partnership shall cancel its certificate of limited partnership.
(4)  A conversion takes effect when the certificate of limited partnership is canceled.
(5)  A limited partner who becomes a general partner as a result of a conversion remains liable only as a limited partner for an obligation incurred by the limited partnership before the conversion takes effect. The partner is liable as a general partner for an obligation of the partnership incurred after the conversion takes effect.

**Section 51.    Effect of conversion; entity unchanged.**
(1)  A partnership or limited partnership that has been converted pursuant to s. 49 or s. 55 is for all purposes the same entity that existed before the conversion.
(2)  When a conversion takes effect:
  (a)  Title to all personal property owned by the converting partnership or limited partnership remains vested in the converted entity. Title to all real property owned by the converting partnership or limited partnership shall be transferred by deed to the converted entity; and
  (b)  All liabilities and obligations of the converting partnership or limited partnership continue as liabilities and obligations of the converted entity.
(3)  A claim existing or action or proceeding pending by or against a converting partnership or limited partnership may be continued as if the conversion had not occurred.
(4)  Neither the rights of creditors of a converting partnership or limited partnership nor any liens upon the property of a converting partnership or limited partnership are impaired by a conversion.

**Section 52.    Merger of partnerships.**

*[text omitted]*

**Section 53.    Effect of merger.**

*[text omitted]*

**Section 54.    Statement of merger.**

*[text omitted]*

**Section 55.    Nonexclusive.**
Sections 48 - 54 are not exclusive. Partnerships or limited partnerships may be converted or merged in any other manner provided by law.

## LOUISIANA PARTNERSHIP ACT

**Art. 2801.     Partnership; definition**

A partnership is a juridical person, distinct from its partners, created by a contract between two or more persons to combine their efforts or resources in determined proportions and to collaborate at mutual risk for their common profit or commercial benefit.

Trustees and succession representatives, in their capacities as such, and unincorporated associations may be partners.

**Art. 2802.     Applicability of rules or conventional obligations**

The contract of partnership is governed by the provisions in the Title: Of Conventional Obligations, in all matters that are not otherwise provided for by this Title.

**Art. 2803.     Participation of partners**

Each partner participates equally in profits, commercial benefits, and losses of the partnership, unless the partners have agreed otherwise. The same rule applies to the distribution of assets, but in the absence of contrary agreement, contributions to capital are restored to each partner according to the contribution made.

**Art. 2804.     Participation in one category only**

If a partnership agreement establishes the extent of participation by partners in only one category of either profits, commercial benefits, losses, or the distribution of assets other than capital contributions, partners participate to that extent in each category unless the agreement itself or the nature of the participation indicates the partners intend otherwise.

**Art. 2805.     Name of the partnership**

A partnership may adopt a name with or without the inclusion of the names of any of the partners. If no name is adopted, the business must be conducted in the name of all the partners.

**Art. 2806.     The ownership of immovable property**

An immovable acquired in the name of a partnership is owned by the partnership if, at the time of acquisition, the contract of partnership was in writing. If the contract of partnership was not in writing at the time of acquisition, the immovable is owned by the partners.

As to third parties, the individual partners shall be deemed to own immovable property acquired in the name of the partnership until the contract of partnership is filed for registry with the secretary of state as provided by law.

**Art. 2807.     Decisions affecting the partnership**

Unless otherwise agreed, unanimity is required to amend the partnership agreement, to admit new partners, to terminate the partnership, or to permit a partner to withdraw without just cause if the partnership has been constituted for a term.

Decisions affecting the management or operation of a partnership must be made by a majority of the partners, but the parties may stipulate otherwise.

**Art. 2808.     Obligation of a partner to contribute**

Each partner owes the partnership all that he has agreed to contribute to it.

**Art. 2809.     Fiduciary duty; activities prejudicial to the partnership**

A partner owes a fiduciary duty to the partnership and to his partners. He may not conduct any activity, for himself or on behalf of a third person, that is contrary to his fiduciary duty and is prejudicial to the partnership. If he does so, he must account to the partnership and to his partners for the resulting profits.

**Art. 2810.     Other rights not prejudiced**

The provisions of Article 2808 and 2809 do not prejudice other rights granted by law to recover damages or to obtain injunctive relief in appropriate cases.

**Art. 2811.        Partner as creditor of the partnership**

A partner who acts in good faith for the partnership may be a creditor of the partnership for sums he disburses, obligations he incurs, and losses he sustains thereby.

**Art. 2812.        The sharing of a partner's interest with a third person**

A partner may share his interest in the partnership with a third person without the consent of his partners, but he cannot make him a member of the partnership. He is responsible for damage to the partnership caused by the third person as though he caused it himself.

**Art. 2813.        The right of a partner to obtain information**

A partner may inform himself of the business activities of the partnership and may consult its books and records, even if he has been excluded from management. A contrary agreement is null.

He may not exercise his right in a manner that unduly interferes with the operations of the partnership or prevents other partners from exercising their rights in this regard.

**Art. 2814.        Partner as mandatary of the partnership**

A partner is a mandatary of the partnership for all matters in the ordinary course of its business other than the alienation, lease, or encumbrance of its immovables. A provision that a partner is not a mandatary does not affect third persons who in good faith transact business with the partner. Except as provided in the articles of partnership, any person authorized to execute a mortgage or security agreement on behalf of a partnership shall, for purposes of executory process, have authority to execute a confession of judgment in the act of mortgage or security agreement without execution of the articles of partnership by authentic act.

**Art. 2815.        Effect of loss stipulation on third parties**

A provision that a partner shall not participate in losses does not affect third parties.

**Art. 2816.        Contract by partner in his own name; effect on the partnership**

An obligation contracted for the partnership by a partner in his own name binds the partnership if the partnership benefits by the transaction or the transaction involves matters in the ordinary course of its business. If the partnership is so bound, it can enforce the contract in its own name.

**Art. 2817.        Partnership debts; liability**

A partnership as principal obligor is primarily liable for its debts. A partner is bound for his virile share of the debts of the partnership but may plead discussion of the assets of the partnership.

**Art. 2818.        Causes of cessation of membership**

A partner ceases to be a member of a partnership upon: his death or interdiction; his being granted an order for relief under Chapter 7 of the Bankruptcy Code; his interest in the partnership being seized and not released as provided in Article 2819; his expulsion from the partnership; or his withdrawal from the partnership.

A partner also ceases to be a member of a partnership in accordance with the provisions of the contract of partnership.

**Art. 2819.        Seizure of the interest of a partner**

A partner ceases to be a member of a partnership if his interest in the partnership is seized under a writ of execution and is not released within thirty days. The cessation is retroactive to the date of seizure.

**Art. 2820.        Expulsion of a partner for just cause**

A partnership may expel a partner for just cause. Unless otherwise provided in the partnership agreement, a majority of the partners must agree on the expulsion.

**Art. 2821.        Partnership constituted for term; withdrawal**

If a partnership has been constituted for a term, a partner may withdraw without the consent of his partners prior to the expiration of the term provided he has just cause arising out of the failure of another partner to perform an obligation.

**Art. 2822.** **Partnership without term; withdrawal**

If a partnership has been constituted without a term, a partner may withdraw from the partnership without the consent of his partners at any time, provided he gives reasonable notice in good faith at a time that is not unfavorable to the partnership.

**Art. 2823.** **Rights of a partner after withdrawal**

The former partner, his successors, or the seizing creditor is entitled to an amount equal to the value that the share of the former partner had at the time membership ceased.

**Art. 2824.** **Payment of interest of partner**

If a partnership continues to exist after the membership of a partner ceases, unless otherwise agreed, the partnership must pay in money the amount referred to in Article 2823 as soon as that amount is determined together with interest at the legal rate from the time membership ceases.

**Art. 2825.** **Judicial determination of amount**

If there is no agreement on the amount to be paid under Articles 2823 and 2824, any interested party may seek a judicial determination of the amount and a judgment ordering its payment.

**Art. 2826.** **Termination of a partnership; causes**

Unless continued as provided by law, a partnership is terminated by: the unanimous consent of its partners; a judgment of termination; the granting of an order for relief to the partnership under Chapter 7 of the Bankruptcy Code; the reduction of its membership to one person; the expiration of its term; or the attainment of, or the impossibility or attainment of the object of the partnership.

A partnership also terminates in accordance with provisions of the contract of partnership.

A partnership in commendam, however, terminates by the retirement from the partnership, or the death, interdiction, or dissolution, of the sole or any general partner unless the partnership is continued with the consent of the remaining general partners under a right to do so stated in the contract of partnership or if, within ninety days after such event, all the remaining partners agree in writing to continue the partnership and to the appointment of one or more general partners if necessary or desired.

**Art. 2827.** **Continuation of a partnership**

A partnership may be expressly or tacitly continued when its term expires or its object is attained, or when a resultory condition of the contract of partnership is fulfilled. If the object becomes impossible, the partnership may be continued for a different object.

Unless otherwise agreed, a partnership that is expressly or tacitly continued has not term.

**Art. 2828.** **Continuation for liquidation; sole proprietorship**

When a partnership terminates, the business of the partnership ends except for purposes of liquidation.

If a partnership terminates because its membership is reduced to one person, that person is not bound to liquidate the partnership and may continue the business as a sole proprietor. If the person elects to continue the business, his former partners are entitled to amounts equal to the value of their shares as of time the partnership terminated, and they have the right to demand security for the payment of partnership debts.

**Art. 2829.** **Change in number or identity of partners**

A change in the number or identity of partners does not terminate a partnership unless the number is reduced to one.

**Art. 2830.** **Effects of termination; authority of partners**

When a partnership terminates, the authority of the partners to act for it ceases, except with regard to acts necessary to liquidate its affairs.

Anything done in what would have been the usual course of business of the partnership by a partner acting in good faith, who is unaware that the partnership has terminated, binds the partnership as if it still existed.

**Art. 2831.** **Termination of the partnership; rights of third parties**

The termination of a partnership, for any reason, does not affect the rights of a third person in good faith who transacts business with a partnership or a mandatary acting on behalf of the former partnership.

# APPENDIX C: FORMS

This appendix contains several standard forms. If none of these forms fit your situation, or the agreement between you and your partners, you will need to prepare a custom form. This can either be done by making the necessary changes in the forms in this appendix, or by selecting the clauses you need from the various clauses in Appendix D and preparing a custom agreement.

This appendix contains the following forms (page numbers are given for where each form begins):

*The **AMENDMENT TO PARTNERSHIP AGREEMENT** (form 5) can be used in an unlimited number of situations, whenever it is necessary or desirable to change the terms of the partnership agreement.

# PARTNERSHIP AGREEMENT

This Partnership Agreement is entered into this _____ day of _____,_____, by and between the following partners: _____
_____
_____

who agree as follows:

    **1.    Name of Partnership.** The name of the partnership shall be: _____
_____. The name under which the partnership shall conduct business shall be: _____.

    **2.    Principal Place of Business.** The partnership's principal place of business shall be:
_____

    **3.    Purpose of Partnership.** The purposes of the partnership are: _____
_____.

    In addition to the specific purposes set forth above, the purpose of the partnership is also to conduct any lawful business in which the partners, from time to time, may agree to become engaged.

    **4.    Term of Partnership.** The partnership shall become effective as of the date of this agreement, and shall continue until it is dissolved by all of the partners, or until otherwise dissolved by law.

    **5.    Contribution of Partners.** Each partner shall make an initial cash contribution to the partnership in the amount of $_____.

    **6.    Profits and Losses / Ownership Interests.** The partners shall share equally in the profits and losses of the partnership.

    **7.    Voting Rights.** All partnership decisions must be made by the unanimous agreement of the partners. All matters not referred to in this agreement shall be determined according to this paragraph.

    **8.    Transfer of a Partner's Interest.**

    **A.    Option Of Partnership To Purchase / Right Of First Refusal.** In the event either partner leaves the partnership, for whatever reason including voluntary withdrawal or retirement, incapacity, or death, the remaining partner shall have the option to purchase said partner's interest from said partner or his or her estate. In the event any partner receives, and is willing to accept, an offer from a person who is not a partner to purchase all of his or her interest in the partnership, he or she shall notify the other partner of the identity of the proposed buyer, the amount and terms of the offer, and of his or her willingness to accept the offer. The other partner shall then have the option, within 30 days after notice is given, to purchase that partner's interest in the partnership on the same terms as those of the offer of the person who is not a partner, or to put the business up for sale, or to dissolve the partnership.

**B.    Valuation of Partnership.** In the event the remaining partner exercises the right to purchase the other's interest as provided above, the value of the partnership shall be net worth of the partnership as of the date of such purchase. Net worth shall be determined by the market value of the following assets: all of the partnership's real and personal property, liquid assets, accounts receivable, earned but unbilled fees, and money earned for work in progress; less the total amount of all debts owed by the partnership.

**C.    Payment Upon Buy-Out.** In the event the remaining partner exercises the right to purchase the other's interest as provided above, the remaining partner shall pay the departing partner for his or her interest by way of a promissory note of the partnership, dated as of the date of purchase, which shall mature in not more than _____ years, and shall bear interest at the rate of _____% per annum. The first payment shall be made _____ days after the date of the promissory note.

**9.    Governing Law.** This agreement shall be governed by the laws of _____.

**10.    Severability.** If any part of this agreement is adjudged invalid, illegal, or unenforceable, the remaining parts shall not be affected and shall remain in full force and effect.

**11.    Binding Agreement / No Other Beneficiary.** This agreement shall be binding upon the parties, and upon their heirs, executors, personal representatives, administrators, and assigns. No person shall have a right or cause of action arising or resulting from this agreement except those who are parties to it and their successors in interest.

**12.    Entire Agreement.** This instrument, including any attached exhibits, constitutes the entire agreement of the parties. No representations or promises have been made except those that are set out in this agreement. This agreement may not be modified except in writing signed by the parties.

**13.    Paragraph Headings.** The headings of the paragraphs contained in this agreement are for convenience only, and are not to be considered a part of this agreement or used in determining its content or context.

_____          _____
Signature                                                      Signature

_____          _____
Signature                                                      Signature

_____          _____
Signature                                                      Signature

# PARTNERSHIP AGREEMENT

This Partnership Agreement is entered into this _____ day of _____, _____, by and between the following partners: _____

_____

_____who agree as follows:

1. **Name of Partnership.** The name of the partnership shall be:

_____.

The name under which the partnership shall conduct business shall be:

_____.

2. **Principal Place of Business.** The partnership's principal place of business shall be:

_____.

3. **Purpose of Partnership.** The purposes of the partnership are: _____

_____.

In addition to the specific purposes set forth above, the purpose of the partnership is also to conduct any lawful business in which the partners, from time to time, may agree to become engaged.

4. **Term of Partnership.** The partnership shall become effective as of the date of this agreement, and shall continue until it is dissolved by all of the partners, or until a partner leaves for any reason including incapacity or death, or until otherwise dissolved by law.

5. **Contributions of Partners.** The partners shall make the following initial contributions to the partnership:

| Partner | Type of Contribution | Value |
|---|---|---|
| _____ | _____ | _____ |
| _____ | _____ | _____ |
| _____ | _____ | _____ |
| _____ | _____ | _____ |
| _____ | _____ | _____ |
| _____ | _____ | _____ |

6. **Loans of Cash.** The following partners agree to loan the partnership the amount listed below, for the period of time and at the annual interest rate stated:

| Partner | Amount | Period | Interest Rate |
|---|---|---|---|
| _____ | _____ | _____ | _____ |
| _____ | _____ | _____ | _____ |
| _____ | _____ | _____ | _____ |
| _____ | _____ | _____ | _____ |
| _____ | _____ | _____ | _____ |
| _____ | _____ | _____ | _____ |

7. **Loans of Property.** The following partners agree to loan the partnership the property listed below, which shall remain the property of such partner and shall be returned to that partner upon termination of the partnership unless another time for return is specified:

| Partner | Description of Property |
|---------|-------------------------|
| _____ | _____ |
| _____ | _____ |
| _____ | _____ |
| _____ | _____ |
| _____ | _____ |
| _____ | _____ |

**8.  Additional Contributions.** No additional funds shall be required of any partner, unless the partners unanimously vote to contribute additional funds. In the event additional funds are needed, and a unanimous vote is not achieved, those partners desiring to continue the business may purchase the interest of any partner not desiring to make further contributions; or may make contributions with the ownership and voting rights of the partners being adjusted according to each partner's total contributions; otherwise the partnership shall be terminated and wound-up.

**9.  Profits and Losses.** The partners shall share in the profits and losses of the partnership according to the following percentages:

| Partner | % of Profits | % of Losses |
|---------|--------------|-------------|
| _____ | _____ | _____ |
| _____ | _____ | _____ |
| _____ | _____ | _____ |
| _____ | _____ | _____ |
| _____ | _____ | _____ |
| _____ | _____ | _____ |

**A.  Distribution of Profits.** Any profits to which a partner shall be entitled, shall be determined and paid on a monthly basis.

**B.  Limitation on Distribution of Profits.** Upon the majority vote of the partners, some or all of the total partnership profits shall be retained by the partnership for reinvestment in the partnership business, with the balance, if any, being distributed among the partners.

**10. Ownership Interests.** Each partner's share of ownership in the partnership, with voting rights equal to each partner's percentage, shall be as follows:

| Partner | % of Ownership |
|---------|----------------|
| _____ | _____ |
| _____ | _____ |

| Partner | % of Ownership |
|---------|----------------|
| _____ | _____ |
| _____ | _____ |
| _____ | _____ |

**11. Voting Rights.** All partnership decisions shall be made by a majority vote of the partners. Each partner shall have a certain number of votes, which shall be equal to his or her percentage of ownership in the partnership as set forth in this agreement. In the event any proposal does not receive a majority vote, that proposal shall be deemed defeated.

**12. Participation in Partnership Business.** Each partner shall participate in the partnership business in the following capacity:

Partner                                    Capacity

_____          _____
_____          _____
_____          _____
_____          _____
_____          _____
_____          _____

Each partner shall work a minimum of _____ hours per week in the partnership business, provided that each partner shall be entitled to the following vacation, sick, and holiday leaves:

Vacation:       _____
Sick Leave:    _____
Holidays:       _____

**13. Salaries to Partners.** Partners may be paid a reasonable salary or wages for work performed in the partnership business, but only as determined in writing by a majority vote of the partners.

**14. Partnership Accounting Records.** The partnership shall maintain proper and complete accounting records, in accordance with generally accepted accounting principals. Such records shall be kept at the partnership's principal place of business, and shall be available and open to all partners, or their representatives, for inspection at any time during regular business hours.

**15. Accounting to Partners.** An accounting of the partnership business, including profits and losses, shall be made to all partners at the close of each quarter. In addition, an accounting shall be made at any time upon the written request of any partner.

**16. Partnership Bank Accounts.** The partnership shall maintain at least one bank checking account, which shall bear the partnership name. Other bank accounts may be maintained as determined necessary by the partners, however, all such accounts shall bear the partnership name. All partnership funds shall only be deposited in accounts bearing the partnership name. All checks drawn on partnership checking accounts must be signed by at least _____ partners. All withdrawals of funds from other partnership accounts must be on the signature of at least _____ partners.

**17. Expense Accounts.** The partners listed below shall receive a monthly expense account in the amount indicated for actual, necessary and reasonable expenses incurred in the regular course of partnership business. Each such partner shall keep a record of his or her expenses, and shall submit such record monthly for payment.

| Partner | Amount | Partner | Amount |
|---------|--------|---------|--------|
| _____ | _____ | _____ | _____ |
| _____ | _____ | _____ | _____ |
| _____ | _____ | _____ | _____ |

### 18. Insurance.

**A.    Insurance of Business.** The partnership shall maintain policies of insurance to cover liability and business assets. Business asset insurance shall be sufficient to replace such assets. Liability insurance shall be in an amount determined by a majority vote of partners.

**B.    Life Insurance on Partners.** The partnership shall maintain a life insurance policy on each partner in the face value of $_____. Said policy shall be an asset of the partnership.

**C.    Disability Insurance on Partners.** The partnership shall maintain a disability insurance policy on each partner in the face value of $_____. Said policy shall be an asset of the partnership.

### 19. Partnership Meetings.
In order to discuss partnership business, the partners shall meet _____, or at such other times as determined by a majority vote of the partners.

### 20. Transfer of Partner's Interest in Partnership.

**A.    Option of Partnership to Purchase / Right of First Refusal.** In the event any partner leaves the partnership, for whatever reason including voluntary withdrawal or retirement, expulsion, incapacity, or death, the remaining partner(s) shall have the option to purchase said partner's interest from said partner or his or her estate. In the event any partner receives, and is willing to accept, an offer from a person who is not a partner to purchase all of his or her interest in the partnership, he or she shall notify the other partners of the identity of the proposed buyer, the amount and terms of the offer, and of his or her willingness to accept the offer. The other partner(s) shall then have the option, within 30 days after notice is given, to purchase that partner's interest in the partnership on the same terms as those of the offer of the person who is not a partner.

**B.    Option of Partnership to Sell or Dissolve Partnership.** In the event a partner leaves or receives an offer to purchase his or her interest as provided for in Paragraph 20. A., above, and the remaining partner(s) do not exercise the option to purchase, the remaining partners have the option to put the entire business up for sale, or to dissolve the partnership.

**C.    Valuation of Partnership.** In the event the remaining partners exercise their right to purchase another partner's interest as provided above, the value of the partnership shall be determined by an independent appraisal. The cost of the appraisal shall be shared equally by the departing partner and the partnership.

**D.    Payment Upon Buy-Out.** In the event the remaining partners exercise their right to purchase another partner's interest as provided above, they shall pay the departing partner for his or her interest by way of a promissory note of the partnership, dated as of the date of purchase, which shall mature in not more than _____ years, and shall bear interest at the rate of _____% per annum. The first payment shall be made _____ days after the date of the promissory note.

### 21. Expulsion of a Partner.
A partner shall be expelled from the partnership for any of the following reasons:

a.    Upon a unanimous vote of the other partners to expel a partner.
b.    When the partner files a petition for relief under the Bankruptcy Code.
c.    When the partner files for, or becomes subject to an order or decree of, insolvency under

any state law.

d.   When the partner files for, consents to, or becomes subject to, the appointment of a receiver or trustee over any of his or her assets which is not vacated within _____ days.

e.   When the partner consents to, or becomes subject to, an attachment or execution of his or her assets which is not released within _____ days.

f.   When the partner makes an assignment for the benefit of creditors.

Upon the occurrence of any of the above events, the expelled partner shall cease to be a partner and shall have no interest in the partnership or partnership property. Said partner's rights, powers and authorities, including the right to share in partnership profits, shall also cease. The expelled partner shall be considered a seller of his or her interest in the partnership as set forth in this agreement. In the event of any such expulsion, the partnership shall not be dissolved, but shall continue its business without interruption. The expulsion of any partner as provided above shall not be subject to mediation, arbitration, or review by any court.

**22.  Partnership Business Name.** The business name of the partnership, _____ _____, is owned by the partnership. No partner may use said name after leaving the partnership.

**23.  Ownership of Trade Secrets.** All trade secrets used or developed by the partnership, including customer lists, supply sources, and computer programs, shall be owned and controlled by the partnership.

**24.  Dispute Resolution.**

   **A.  Mediation of Disputes.** In the event of any dispute arising under this agreement, all partners agree that a resolution shall first be sought through mediation. As mediation is voluntary, all partners agree to cooperate with the mediator in attempting to resolve the dispute. It is agreed that _____ shall serve as mediator, and that if such person is unable or unwilling to serve as mediator another mediator shall be chosen by mutual agreement of the partners to the dispute. Mediation shall be initiated by a written request for mediation, which shall be delivered to the other partners and the mediator. Mediation shall commence within _____ days after the request for mediation is delivered. Any agreement reached at through mediation shall be reduced to writing, shall be signed by all of the partners, and shall be binding upon all of the partners. Any costs of mediation shall be shared equally by all partners to the dispute.

   **B.  Arbitration.** In the event of any dispute arising under this agreement which could not be resolved through mediation, all partners agree that a resolution shall be sought through arbitration. Arbitration shall be initiated by a written request for arbitration, which shall state the nature of the dispute, the requesting party's position, and shall name one person to serve as an arbitrator. Such request shall be delivered to the other partners. Arbitration shall proceed as follows:

   1.   Within 3 days after receiving the request for arbitration, the other partners shall have the right to deliver a response, which shall name a person to serve as the second arbitrator, and may state the responding partners' position. This response shall be delivered to the other party to the dispute.

   2.   Within 3 days after receiving a copy of the request and the response, the two designated arbitrators shall select a third arbitrator.

   3.   Within 7 days after selection of the third arbitrator, the arbitrators shall hold a hearing, at which time either party may present oral or written evidence. No partner may be represented by an attorney or any other third party.

4. The arbitrators shall issue a written decision within 7 days of the hearing date, which shall be delivered to both parties, and shall be binding upon them.

5. Any costs of arbitration shall be shared equally by all partners to the dispute.

**25. Continuity of Partnership.** In the event of a partner's voluntary withdrawal, expulsion, death, or incapacity, the partnership shall not terminate or dissolve, but shall continue its business without any break in continuity.

**26. Governing Law.** This agreement shall be governed by the laws of _____
_____.

**27. Severability.** If any part of this agreement is adjudged invalid, illegal, or unenforceable, the remaining parts shall not be affected and shall remain in full force and effect.

**28. Binding Agreement / No Other Beneficiary.** This agreement shall be binding upon the parties, and upon their heirs, executors, personal representatives, administrators, and assigns. No person shall have a right or cause of action arising or resulting from this agreement except those who are parties to it and their successors in interest.

**29. Entire Agreement.** This instrument, including any attached exhibits, constitutes the entire agreement of the parties. No representations or promises have been made except those that are set out in this agreement. This agreement may not be modified except in writing signed by all the parties.

**30. Paragraph Headings.** The headings of the paragraphs contained in this agreement are for convenience only, and are not to be considered a part of this agreement or used in determining its content or context.

_____      _____
Signature                                     Signature

_____      _____
Signature                                     Signature

_____      _____
Signature                                     Signature

# PARTNERSHIP TERMINATION AGREEMENT

This Partnership Termination Agreement is entered into this _____ day of _____, _____, by and between the following partners: _____
_____,
who agree as follows:

### 1.    Partnership.

The above named parties have been and are now partners doing business pursuant to a Partnership Agreement dated _____, under the name of _____, with its principal place of business in
_____.

### 2.    Agreement To Dissolve Partnership.

The partners hereby agree to dissolve their partnership and liquidate its affairs, according to the provisions of this agreement.

### 3.    Valuation of Partnership Assets.

The partners agree that each partnership asset has a present fair market value equal to its book value to the partnership as reflected on the partnership financial records, unless any such asset is sold in which event that asset shall be deemed to have a value equal to its sale price.

### 4.    Termination of Partnership Business.

After _____, _____, no partner shall do any further business nor incur any further obligations on behalf of the partnership. except for the purposes of carrying out the liquidation of the partnership and the winding-up of partnership affairs.

### 5.    Liquidation.

Liquidation of the partnership shall proceed as follows:

### A.    Accounting.

The partnership accountant shall perform an accounting of all assets and liabilities of the partnership, and of the respective equities of the creditors and the partners in the assets, as of the date such

accounting is performed. Such accounting shall be performed no later than _____,
_____.

### B.   Settling Accounts.

Upon completion of the accounting, the partners shall pay all of the liabilities of the partnership, including those owing to the partners other than for capital contributions. Payment of liabilities owing to the partners shall include payment of profits for the current accounting period computed on the basis of actual cash receipts through the date of the accounting. Any funds received after the date of the accounting shall be distributed among the partners according to each partner's percentage of ownership in the partnership.

### C.   Distribution of Partnership Assets.

Any partnership assets remaining after payment of all partnership liabilities shall be sold, with the proceeds being divided among the partners according to each partner's percentage of ownership in the partnership. Each partner shall have the right to purchase any partnership asset at book value, before any sale to a non-partner. The following assets shall be transferred to individual partners as their individual property as indicated below:

| Asset | Book Value | Partner Becoming Owner |
|---|---|---|
| _____ | _____ | _____ |
| _____ | _____ | _____ |
| _____ | _____ | _____ |
| _____ | _____ | _____ |

## 6.   Disclosure.

Except as appears in the books of the partnership, each of the partners represents that he or she has not heretofore contracted any liability that can or may charge the partnership or the other partner, nor has he or she received or discharged any of the credits, monies or effects of the partnership.

## 7.   Partnership Name.

No partner shall use the partnership's name or any name confusingly similar thereto in any new business activity for a period of _____. Until that time any partner shall be entitled to refer to the partnership name solely for purposes of a transition from the partnership to his or her new business, or to the extent necessary to explain such partner's employment and work history.

## 8.   Governing Law.

This agreement shall be governed by the laws of _____.

**9. Binding Agreement / No Other Beneficiary.**

This agreement shall be binding upon the parties, and upon their heirs, executors, personal representatives, administrators, and assigns. No person shall have a right or cause of action arising or resulting from this agreement except those who are parties to it and their successors in interest.

**10. Entire Agreement.**

This instrument, including any attached exhibits, constitutes the entire agreement of the parties with respect to the termination of the partnership. No representations or promises have been made except those that are set out in this agreement. This agreement may not be modified except in writing signed by all the parties.

_____     _____

_____     _____

_____     _____

*This page intentionally left blank.*

# PARTNERSHIP BUY-OUT AGREEMENT

This Partnership Buy-Out Agreement is entered into this _____ day of _____, _____, by and between _____, (hereinafter referred to as "Seller"), and _____ _____, (hereinafter referred to as "Buyers"), who agree as follows:

**1.    Partnership.** The above named parties hereto have been and are now partners doing business pursuant to a Partnership Agreement dated _____, under the name of _____, with its principal place of business in _____.

**2.    Agreement to Purchase and Sell.** The Buyers hereby agree to purchase, and the Seller hereby agrees to sell, all of the Seller's interest in the partnership according to the terms of this Partnership Buy-Out Agreement.

**3.    Valuation.** The parties agree that each partnership asset has a present fair market value equal to its book value to the partnership as reflected in the partnership financial records, and that any consideration in this agreement which is in excess of book value is attributable to goodwill not shown in the partnership financial records.

**4.    Purchase.** The Buyers hereby purchase, and the Seller hereby sells, all of the Seller's interest in the partnership and partnership property, in consideration of:

a.    The payment to the Seller of $_____, to be paid:

❏ In full in cash, check or money order, to be paid within 30 days after the date of this agreement.

❏ A negotiable promissory note in the form of Exhibit A attached hereto.

❏ The sum of $_____ to be paid in cash within 30 days after the date of this agreement, and a negotiable promissory note for the balance in the form of Exhibit A attached hereto.

b.    The agreement of the Buyer's and the partnership to hold the Seller free and harmless from all partnership debts and liabilities.

**5.    Amendment of Partnership Agreement.** The Partnership Agreement is hereby amended to provide that from and after the date of this agreement, only the Buyers shall exercise management and control over partnership decisions, and that from and after that date, the ownership, profits and losses of the partnership will be shared by the Buyers as follows:

| Partner | % Ownership | % Profits | % Losses |
|---|---|---|---|
| _____ | _____ | _____ | _____ |
| _____ | _____ | _____ | _____ |
| _____ | _____ | _____ | _____ |
| _____ | _____ | _____ | _____ |
| _____ | _____ | _____ | _____ |

**6.   Competition Permitted.** From and after _____, _____, the Seller shall be free to conduct consulting activities apart from the partnership, even to the extent of competing with the partnership.

**7.   Insurance.** The Seller shall be entitled to assume the life insurance policy on his or her life presently carried by the partnership, but shall be required to maintain all future premium payments. The Seller shall continue to receive insurance coverage under the partnership's policies as follows:

| Type of Insurance | Coverage Termination Date |
|---|---|
| _____ | _____ |
| _____ | _____ |
| _____ | _____ |

**8.   Partnership Name.** The Seller shall not use the partnership's name or any name confusingly similar thereto in any new business activity conducted by him or her. The Seller may refer to the partnership name solely for purposes of indicating transition from the partnership to his or her new business, or to the extent necessary to identify prior projects that the Seller has completed.

**9.   Disclosure.** Except as appears by the books of the partnership, each of the partners represents that he or she has not heretofore contracted any liability that can or may charge the partnership or any other partner, nor has he or she received or discharged any of the credits, monies or effects of the partnership.

**10.   Continuity of Partnership.** After the Seller's departure from the partnership, the partnership shall not terminate or dissolve, but shall continue its business without any break in continuity.

**11.   Governing Law.** This agreement shall be governed by the laws of _____ _____.

**12.   Binding Agreement / No Other Beneficiary.** This agreement shall be binding upon the parties, and upon their heirs, executors, personal representatives, administrators, and assigns. No person shall have a right or cause of action arising or resulting from this agreement except those who are parties to it and their successors in interest.

**13. Entire Agreement.** This instrument, including any attached exhibits, constitutes the entire agreement of the parties with respect to this buy-out. No representations or promises have been made except those that are set out in this agreement. This agreement may not be modified except in writing signed by all the parties.

_____
Signature

_____
Signature

_____
Signature

_____
Signature

_____
Signature

_____
Signature

*This page intentionally left blank.*

## AMENDMENT TO PARTNERSHIP AGREEMENT

This Amendment to Partnership Agreement is entered into on _____,
_____, by and between _____
_____,
who agree as follows:

1.    The Partnership Agreement for _____, dated
_____, is hereby amended to read as follows:

2.    In all other respects not referred to herein, said Partnership Agreement is ratified and confirmed, and shall remain in full force and effect.

_____          _____
Signature                                         Signature

_____          _____
Signature                                         Signature

*This page intentionally left blank.*

## PARTNERSHIP AGREEMENT

This Partnership Agreement is entered into this _____ day of _____, _____, by and between the following partners: _____ _____ _____who agree as follows:

1. **Name of Partnership.** The name of the partnership shall be: _____ _____.

2. **Principal Place of Business.** The partnership's principal place of business shall be: _____.

3. **Purpose of Partnership.** The purpose of the partnership is to invest assets of the partnership in stocks, bonds, and securities for the education and benefit of the partners.

4. **Term of Partnership.** The partnership shall become effective as of the date of this agreement, and shall continue until it is dissolved by all of the partners or by law. In the event of a partner's voluntary withdrawal, expulsion, death, or incapacity, the partnership shall not terminate or dissolve, but shall continue its business without any break in continuity.

5. **Contributions of Partners.** Each partner shall make a contribution to the partnership in the amount of $_____ per month, to be paid at each monthly meeting to the Financial Partner by cash or check in the partnership's name, to be used for investing in stocks, bonds, or securities. Each partner shall also contribute the sum of $_____ at the first meeting of each year, for administrative expenses. No additional funds shall be required of any partner, unless the partners unanimously vote to contribute additional funds.

6. **Delinquent Contributions.** Any partner who does not make a contribution required by paragraph 5 within 30 days after it is due, shall be subject to a late fee in the amount of $_____, which shall be deposited in the partnership's bank account.

7. **Capital Accounts.** A capital account shall be maintained in the name of each partner. Each partner's monthly contribution shall be credited to that partner's capital account. Any increase or decrease in the value of the partnership as of any valuation date shall be proportionally credited or debited to each partner's capital account on the valuation date.

8. **Profits and Losses.** The partners shall share in the profits and losses according to the relative percentage of the credit balance in each partner's capital account.

9. **Valuation.** The value of the partnership at any time shall be determined as of the date of the last broker's statement (the "valuation date"), and shall be the value of the assets and property of the partnership on the valuation date, less the value of the debts and liabilities of the partnership on the valuation date.

**10. Voting Rights**. Partnership decisions shall be made by a 2/3 majority vote of the partners, unless otherwise provided in this agreement. Each partner shall have a number of votes equal to the relative percentage of the credit balance in his or her capital account. In the event any proposal does not receive a 2/3 majority vote, that proposal shall be deemed defeated. An absent partner may execute a proxy authorizing another partner to cast his or her vote(s), however, no more than one proxy may be accepted or voted by a partner.

**11. Officers**. There shall be a Presiding Partner, Assistant Partner, Recording Partner, and Financial Partner, who will be elected annually. Elections shall be held at the first meeting for the first year, and at the regular December meetings for all subsequent years. Officers may succeed themselves in the same office. Said officers shall have the following duties:

**Presiding Partner:** The Presiding Partner shall preside at meetings, appoint a parliamentarian, appoint committees, and generally oversee activities of the partnership.

**Assistant Partner.** The Assistant Partner shall assume the duties of the Presiding Partner when the Presiding Partner is absent or temporarily unable to carry out his or her duties.

**Recording Partner.** The Recording Partner shall keep a record of partnership activities and report on previous meetings.

**Financial Partner.** The Financial Partner shall collect and disburse funds, maintain books of the partnership's financial operations, assets, and partner's capital accounts; issue receipts for partner's contributions; prepare statements of the value of the partnership when required; prepare proper tax forms and provide tax information to partners; and coordinate buy and sell orders with the broker on instructions from the partners.

**12. No Compensation of Partners.** No partner may be compensated for services rendered to the partnership, except to reimbursement for authorized expenses.

**13. Partnership Accounting Records.** The partnership shall maintain proper and complete accounting records. Such records shall be kept by the Financial Partner, and shall be available and open to all partners, or their representatives, for inspection at meetings and at any reasonable time by appointment with the Financial Partner. An accounting of the partnership business, including profits and losses, shall be made to all partners annually, and at any other time upon the written request of any partner.

**14. Partnership Bank Accounts.** The partnership shall maintain a checking account at a bank, credit union, or other financial institution selected by the partners, which shall bear the partnership name. All partnership funds shall only be deposited in the partnership account. All checks drawn on the partnership checking account must be signed by the Financial Partner or any other partner authorized by the partners to sign checks.

**15. Broker Accounts.** The partnership may select a broker and enter into such agreements with said broker as required for the purchase or sale of stocks, bonds, and securities. The Financial Partner, or other partner appointed by the partners, shall perform the ministerial functions of giving orders to the broker regarding the purchase or sale of stocks, bonds, and securities for the account of the partnership, but only after such purchases or sales have been approved by a majority vote of the partners.

**16.  Partnership Meetings.** The partners shall meet monthly, on the _____ of each month, or at such other times as determined by a simple majority vote of the partners.

**17.  Death, Incapacity, or Voluntary Withdrawal of a Partner.** Any partner may withdraw from the partnership at any time, by submitting a written notice of his or her intent to withdraw to an officer of the partnership. In the event any partner leaves the partnership due to death, physical or mental incapacity, or voluntarily for any reason, said departing partner shall receive 100% of his or her capital account based on the valuation at the last valuation date, less expenses incurred in liquidating assets to make payment available. The partnership may purchase the departing partner's capital account, sell said capital account to any person acceptable to a 2/3 majority of the remaining partners, or liquidate assets to make payment available. Payment shall be made to the departing partner, or his or her estate if appropriate, within 90 days after an officer of the partnership is notified in writing of the departing partner's death, incapacity, or intent to withdraw.

**18.  Expulsion of a Partner.** A partner shall be expelled from the partnership for any of the following reasons:

a.  Upon a unanimous vote of the other partners to expel a partner.

b.  When the partner files a petition for relief under the Bankruptcy Code.

c.  When the partner files for, or becomes subject to an order or decree of, insolvency under any state law.

d.  When the partner files for, consents to, or becomes subject to, the appointment of a receiver or trustee over any of his or her assets which is not vacated within _____ days.

e.  When the partner consents to, or becomes subject to, an attachment or execution of his or her assets which is not released within _____ days.

f.  When the partner makes an assignment for the benefit of creditors.

g.  When the partner becomes delinquent in the payment of monthly contributions for a period of sixty-one days.

Upon the occurrence of any of the above events, the expelled partner shall cease to be a partner and shall have no interest in the partnership or partnership property. Said partner's rights, powers, and authorities, including the right to share in partnership profits, shall also cease. In the event of any such expulsion, the partnership shall not be dissolved, but shall continue its business without interruption. The expulsion of any partner as provided above shall not be subject to mediation, arbitration, or review by any court.

Any partner who is expelled from the partnership pursuant to paragraph 18 a - f, shall receive _____% of his or her capital account based on the valuation at the last valuation date, less expenses incurred in liquidating assets to make payment available. Any partner who is expelled from the partnership pursuant to paragraph 18 g, shall receive _____% of his or her capital account based on the valuation at the last valuation date, less expenses incurred in liquidating assets to make payment available and less any delinquent contributions. The partnership may purchase the expelled partner's capital account, sell said capital account to any person acceptable to a 2/3 majority of the remaining partners, or liquidate assets to make payment available. Payment shall be made to the departing partner within 90 days after expulsion.

**19. Sale or Transfer of Interest Prohibited.** No partner may sell or otherwise transfer his or her capital account or any interest in the partnership to any other person, including any other partner, without the 2/3 majority vote of the other partners. Any attempt, or notice of an intent, to sell or transfer any interest shall be considered, and treated like, a notice of intent to withdraw under paragraph 17.

**20. Governing Law.** This agreement shall be governed by the laws of _____ _____.

**21. Severability.** If any part of this agreement is adjudged invalid, illegal, or unenforceable, the remaining parts shall not be affected and shall remain in full force and effect.

**22. Binding Agreement / No Other Beneficiary.** This agreement shall be binding upon the parties, and upon their heirs, executors, personal representatives, administrators, and assigns. No person shall have a right or cause of action arising or resulting from this agreement except those who are parties to it and their successors in interest.

**23. Entire Agreement.** This instrument, including any attached exhibits, constitutes the entire agreement of the parties. No representations or promises have been made except those that are set out in this agreement. This agreement may not be modified except in writing signed by all the parties.

_____          _____
Signature                                     Signature


_____          _____
Signature                                     Signature


_____          _____
Signature                                     Signature


_____          _____
Signature                                     Signature


_____          _____
Signature                                     Signature

# APPENDIX D: PARTNERSHIP AGREEMENT CLAUSES

This appendix will help you custom design a partnership agreement to fit your needs. Simply look through each type of clause, choose the clauses that fit your situation, and put them together in an agreement.

You will probably not need to use every type of clause found in this appendix. Select the types of clauses that you want in your **PARTNERSHIP AGREEMENT**.

The following types of clauses are included (page numbers are given):

## BASIC BEGINNING CLAUSES

The paragraphs on this page are a good beginning for all partnership agreements. Use all of the clauses on this page.

---

### PARTNERSHIP AGREEMENT

This Partnership Agreement is entered into this _____ day of _____, _____, by and between the following part-ners: _____

_____,

who agree as follows:

1.    NAME OF PARTNERSHIP. The name of the partnership shall be:

_____.

The name under which the partnership shall conduct business shall be:_____.

2.    PRINCIPAL PLACE OF BUSINESS. The partnership's principal place of business shall be: _____

_____.

3.    PURPOSE OF PARTNERSHIP. The purposes of the partnership are:

_____

_____.

In addition to the specific purposes set forth above, the purpose of the partnership is also to conduct any lawful business in which the partners, from time to time, may agree to become engaged.

## TERM OF PARTNERSHIP

The following are some of many possible variations of clauses describing the term of the partnership. If one of these does not fit your needs, create one that does by combining some of the phrases from the clauses below. Only use *one* Term of Partnership clause.

### *Effective Until Dissolved by All, by Death, or by Law*

**Clause 1**

TERM OF PARTNERSHIP. The partnership shall become effective as of the date of this agreement, and shall continue until it is dissolved by all of the partners, or until a partner leaves for any reason including incapacity or death, or until otherwise dissolved by law.

### *Specific Date of Dissolution*

**Clause 2**

TERM OF PARTNERSHIP. The partnership shall become effective as of the date of this agreement, and shall continue until _____, at which time it shall be dissolved and its affairs wound up.

### *Specific Date of Dissolution Unless Earlier by All, Death, or Law*

**Clause 3**

TERM OF PARTNERSHIP. The partnership shall become effective as of the date of this agreement, and shall continue until _____, at which time it shall be dissolved and its affairs wound up; unless it is earlier dissolved by all of the partners, or a partner leaves for any reason including incapacity or death, or it is otherwise dissolved by law.

### *Specific Effective Date and Dissolution Date*

**Clause 4**

TERM OF PARTNERSHIP. The partnership shall become effective _____, and shall continue until _____, at which time it shall be dissolved and its affairs wound up; unless it is earlier dissolved by all of the partners, or it is otherwise dissolved by law.

## CONTRIBUTIONS

This is a general contributions clause, which allows you to list the type, as well as the amount, of each partner's contribution. See the following three pages for other, more specific, clauses relating to contributions.

CONTRIBUTIONS. The partners shall make the following initial contributions to the partnership:

| Partner | Type of Contribution | Value |
|---------|---------------------|-------|
| _____ | _____ | ____ |
| _____ | _____ | ____ |
| _____ | _____ | ____ |
| _____ | _____ | ____ |

## CASH CONTRIBUTIONS

Only use one of these clauses.

### *Equal Cash Contributions*

*Clause 1*    CASH CONTRIBUTIONS.  Each partner shall make an initial cash contribution to the partnership of $_____.

### *Unequal Cash Contributions*

*Clause 2*    CASH CONTRIBUTIONS.  Each partner shall make the following initial cash contribution to the partnership:

Partner                                                        Amount

_____        _____
_____        _____
_____        _____
_____        _____

## NONCASH CONTRIBUTIONS CLAUSE

Sometimes a partner will contribute something other than cash to start up the partnership. This may be because that partner does not have money to invest, or simply because the property he or she has to contribute is what is needed by the partnership. The following clauses cover various types of noncash items that may be contributed by a partner. If none of these fit your situation, rewrite or combine them as necessary. You may use as many different contribution provisions in your partnership agreement as needed to cover all of the circumstances that apply.

If there will be a contribution of services, you should consult a CPA for any possible tax consequences.

### *Contributions of Property*

*Clause 1*

CONTRIBUTIONS. The following partners shall contribute property to the partnership, of the type and value set forth below:

| Partner | Type of Property | Value |
|---------|------------------|-------|
| _____ | _____ | _____ |
| _____ | _____ | _____ |
| _____ | _____ | _____ |
| _____ | _____ | _____ |

### Miscellaneous Noncash Contributions

**Clause 2** | CONTRIBUTIONS. In addition to, or in place of, cash contributions, the following partners shall contribute the skills, expertise, or work described below to the partnership. Such contributions shall be required in order to equalize the contributions among the partners, and to entitle such partners to their share of interest in the partnership as set forth in this agreement.

| Partner | Description of Contribution | Value |
|---------|----------------------------|-------|
| _____ | _____ | _____ |
| _____ | _____ | _____ |
| _____ | _____ | _____ |
| _____ | _____ | _____ |

### Contribution of Services

**Clause 3** | CONTRIBUTIONS. In addition to, or in place of, cash contributions as stated in this agreement, _____ shall contribute the following services to the partnership for a period of _____, in return for which he or she shall be entitled to _____ percent ownership of the partnership: (specify services)_____.

### Contribution of Use of Intellectual Property

**Clause 4**

CONTRIBUTIONS. The partners listed below shall contribute to the partnership the exclusive use of the listed intellectual property. It is agreed and understood that such partner shall retain sole ownership of his or her intellectual property, which shall not become a partnership asset. It is further agreed that such intellectual property may not be sold, assigned, licensed, or in any way transferred to any third parties by the partnership, without the written consent of the owner of the intellectual property.

| Partner | Description of Intellectual Property | Value |
|---------|--------------------------------------|-------|
| _____ | _____ | _____ |
| _____ | _____ | _____ |
| _____ | _____ | _____ |
| _____ | _____ | _____ |

**NOTE:** *Intellectual property includes such things as patents, copyrights, trademarks, and certain specially designed computer programs.*

### Contribution of Ownership of Intellectual Property

**Clause 5**

CONTRIBUTIONS. In addition to, or in place of, cash contributions, the following partners shall contribute the skills, expertise, or work described below to the partnership. Such contributions shall be required in order to equalize the contributions among the partners, and to entitle such partners to their share of interest in the partnership as set forth in this agreement.

| Partner | Description of Contribution | Value |
|---------|-----------------------------|-------|
| _____ | _____ | _____ |
| _____ | _____ | _____ |
| _____ | _____ | _____ |
| _____ | _____ | _____ |

## ADDITIONAL CONTRIBUTIONS

Sometimes the initial contributions of the partners prove to be insufficient to enable the partnership business to continue after a certain point. This may happen because an insufficient amount was estimated at the beginning, or because economic circumstances have prevented the business from becoming self-supporting as soon as expected.

It may also be desirable for the partners to commit a certain amount of their profits for re-investment in the partnership, in order to finance such things as expansion or replacement of major assets. Only use one of these clauses in your partnership agreement.

Select only one clause from clauses 1, 2 and 3. One of these may be used with either clause 4 or 5 (but do not use both 4 and 5).

### *Majority Vote — Proportional to Each Interest*

*Clause 1*

ADDITIONAL CONTRIBUTIONS. In the event, at any time, more funds are required to carry on the business of the partnership, the necessary capital as determined by a majority vote of the partners shall be provided by the partners in proportion to each partners interest in the partnership as stated in this agreement.

### *Unanimous Vote or Recalculate Interest Percentage*

*Clause 2*

ADDITIONAL CONTRIBUTIONS. No additional funds shall be required of any partner, unless the partners unanimously vote to contribute additional funds. In the event additional funds are needed, and a unanimous vote is not achieved, those partners desiring to continue the business and make the necessary contributions may do so, and each partner's percentage of ownership of the partnership and percentage of share in profits and losses shall be recalculated according to his or her percentage share of the total capital contribution of all partners.

### Unanimous Vote of Purchase Other Partner's Interest

*Clause 3*

ADDITIONAL CONTRIBUTIONS. No additional funds shall be required of any partner, unless the partners unanimously vote to contribute additional funds. In the event additional funds are needed, and a unanimous vote is not achieved, those partners desiring to continue the business may purchase the interest of any partner not desiring to make further contributions; otherwise the partnership shall be terminated and wound-up.

### Annual Contribution by Percentage

*Clause 4*

ADDITIONAL ANNUAL CONTRIBUTIONS. Each partner shall annually contribute _____ percent of his or her share of partnership profits to the partnership, for a period of _____ years.

### Annual Contribution by Amount

*Clause 5*

ADDITIONAL ANNUAL CONTRIBUTIONS. The partners agree to annually contribute to the partnership the amount specified below, for a period of _____ years:

Partner                                             Amount

_____          _____

_____          _____

_____          _____

_____          _____

## LOANS TO PARTNERSHIP BY PARTNERS

Sometimes, in addition to making an outright contribution to the business, a partner will also loan money to the partnership. This may be a loan of money, or of property. You may use both of these clauses if you have partners who are loaning both money and property.

### *Loan of Money*

**Clause 1**

LOAN TO PARTNERSHIP BY PARTNER. The partners listed below agree to loan the partnership money, according to the following terms:

| Partner | Amount of Loan | Interest Rate | Repayment Terms |
| --- | --- | --- | --- |
| _____ | _____ | _____ | _____ |
| _____ | _____ | _____ | _____ |
| _____ | _____ | _____ | _____ |
| _____ | _____ | _____ | _____ |

**NOTE:** *The Interest Rate should list the rate and the term (such as or "1/2 percent per month," or "7% per year," etc.). Repayment Terms should state either when the total amount is to be repaid (such as "Payable in full on July 31, 2005"), or state the amount and frequency of payments (such as "$150 per month beginning March 1, 2004.")*

### *Loan of Property*

**Clause 2**

LOAN TO PARTNERSHIP BY PARTNER. The partners listed below agree to loan to the partnership the following property:

| Partner | Description of Property |
| --- | --- |
| _____ | _____ |
| _____ | _____ |
| _____ | _____ |
| _____ | _____ |

It is agreed and understood by all partners that the above described property shall remain the property of the individual partner, and shall be returned to that partner upon the termination of the partnership, unless an earlier date is set forth above.

## PROFITS AND LOSSES

This clause determines how the profits and losses will be shared between the partners. Only use one of these clauses in your partnership agreement.

### *Equal Share in Profits and Losses*

*Clause 1*

PROFITS AND LOSSES. The partners shall share equally in the profits and losses of the partnership.

### *Proportional Share in Profits and Losses*

*Clause 2*

PROFITS AND LOSSES. Each partner shall share in the profits and losses of the partnership in proportion to each partner's percentage of ownership in the partnership as stated in this agreement.

### *Unequal Shares in Profits and Losses*

*Clause 3*

PROFITS AND LOSSES. The partners shall share in the profits and losses of the partnership according to the following percentages:

| Partner | % of Profits | % of Losses |
|---------|--------------|-------------|
| _____ | _____ | _____ |
| _____ | _____ | _____ |
| _____ | _____ | _____ |
| _____ | _____ | _____ |

# DISTRIBUTION OF PROFITS

These clauses may be separate clauses, or may be added onto the clause on Profits and Losses. These clauses provide more detailed information about when and how any profits are to be given to the partners. Only use one of these clauses in your partnership agreement.

## *When Profits Distributed*

*Clause 1*

DISTRIBUTION OF PROFITS. Any profits to which a partner shall be entitled, shall be determined and paid on a monthly basis.

**NOTE:** *Clause 1 refers to payment of profits on a monthly basis, however, it may be modified if desired to provide for other payment terms, such as monthly, quarterly, annually, etc.*

## *Reinvestment of Profits (Percentage)*

*Clause 2*

LIMITATION ON DISTRIBUTION OF PROFITS. In determining the amount of profits available for distribution to partners, _____% of the total partnership profits shall be retained by the partnership for reinvestment in the partnership business, with the balance being distributed among the partners.

## *Reinvestment of Profits (Dollar Amount)*

*Clause 3*

LIMITATION ON DISTRIBUTION OF PROFITS. In determining the amount of profits available for distribution to partners, the first $_____ of the total partnership profits shall be retained by the partnership for reinvestment in the partnership business, with the balance, if any, being distributed among the partners.

### *Limitation on Distribution of Profits*

**Clause 4**

LIMITATION ON DISTRIBUTION OF PROFITS. Upon the majority vote of the partners, some or all of the total partnership profits shall be retained by the partnership for reinvestment in the partnership business, with the balance, if any, being distributed among the partners.

## OWNERSHIP INTERESTS

This clause determines each partner's share, of percentage, or interest in the partnership business. This clause may also be used to determine each partner's voting rights. Only use one of these clauses in your partnership agreement.

### *Equal Ownership Interests*

*Clause 1*

OWNERSHIP INTERESTS. Each partner shall have an equal share of ownership in the partnership, and an equal vote in partnership decision making authority.

### *Unequal Ownership Interests*

*Clause 2*

OWNERSHIP INTERESTS. Each partner's share of ownership in the partnership, with voting rights equal to each partner's percentage, shall be as follows:

| Partner | % of Ownership |
|---|---|
| _____ | _____ |
| _____ | _____ |
| _____ | _____ |
| _____ | _____ |

# VOTING RIGHTS / DECISION MAKING

This clause determines the voting rights and power of each partner. Only use one of these clauses in your partnership agreement.

### *Unanimous Vote Required*

**Clause 1**

VOTING RIGHTS. All partnership decisions must be made by the unanimous agreement of all partners.

### *Majority Vote Required*

**Clause 2**

VOTING RIGHTS. All partnership decisions shall be made by a majority vote of the partners. Each partner shall have an equal vote with all other partners. In the event any proposal does not receive a majority vote, that proposal shall be deemed defeated.

### *Voting By Percentage of Partnership Interest*

**Clause 3**

VOTING RIGHTS. All partnership decisions shall be made by a majority vote of the partners. Each partner shall have a certain number of votes, which shall be equal to his or her percentage of ownership in the partnership as set forth in this agreement. In the event any proposal does not receive a majority vote, that proposal shall be deemed defeated.

## PARTICIPATION IN PARTNERSHIP BUSINESS

One or more of these clauses may be used in a partnership agreement to indicate each partner's rights and obligations with respect to taking part in the operation of the partnership business. They may be used separately, or combined into one paragraph.

### *General Participation*

*Clause 1*

PARTICIPATION IN PARTNERSHIP BUSINESS. All partners shall be actively involved, and participate, in the operation of the partnership business.

### *Specific Participation*

*Clause 2*

PARTICIPATION IN PARTNERSHIP BUSINESS. Each partner shall participate in the partnership business in the following capacity:

Partner                           Capacity

_____     _____
_____     _____
_____     _____
_____     _____

### *Work Hours and Leave*

*Clause 3*

PARTICIPATION IN PARTNERSHIP BUSINESS. Each partner shall work a minimum of _____ hours per week in the partnership business, provided that each partner shall be entitled to the following vacation, sick, and holiday leaves:
Vacation: _____
Sick Leave: _____
Holidays: _____

## PARTNER SALARIES

Only use one of these clauses in your partnership agreement to set forth the salaries for the partners.

### *No Partner Salaries*

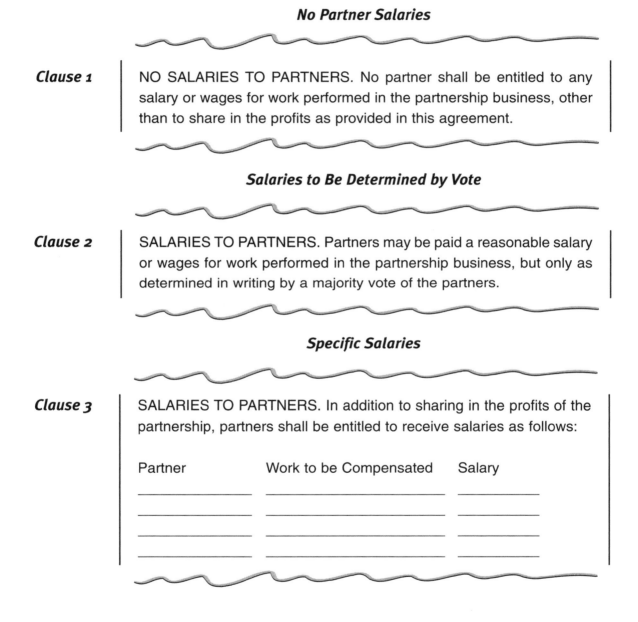

*Clause 1*

NO SALARIES TO PARTNERS. No partner shall be entitled to any salary or wages for work performed in the partnership business, other than to share in the profits as provided in this agreement.

### *Salaries to Be Determined by Vote*

*Clause 2*

SALARIES TO PARTNERS. Partners may be paid a reasonable salary or wages for work performed in the partnership business, but only as determined in writing by a majority vote of the partners.

### *Specific Salaries*

*Clause 3*

SALARIES TO PARTNERS. In addition to sharing in the profits of the partnership, partners shall be entitled to receive salaries as follows:

| Partner | Work to be Compensated | Salary |
|---------|------------------------|--------|
| _____ | _____ | _____ |
| _____ | _____ | _____ |
| _____ | _____ | _____ |
| _____ | _____ | _____ |

# ACCOUNTING

One or more of these may be used in your partnership agreement to set forth various aspects of accounting practices and procedures.

## *Records Available During Business Hours*

*Clause 1*

PARTNERSHIP ACCOUNTING RECORDS. The partnership shall maintain proper and complete accounting records, in accordance with generally accepted accounting principals. Such records shall be kept at the partnership's principal place of business, and shall be available and open to all partners, or their representatives, for inspection at any time during regular business hours.

## *Profits and Losses to Each Partner Quarterly or Upon Request*

*Clause 2*

ACCOUNTING TO PARTNERS. An accounting of the partnership business, including profits and losses, shall be made to all partners at the close of each quarter. In addition, an accounting shall be made at any time upon the written request of any partner.

## *Bank Accounts in Partnership Name*

*Clause 3*

PARTNERSHIP BANK ACCOUNTS. The partnership shall maintain at least one bank checking account, which shall bear the partnership name. Other bank accounts may be maintained as determined necessary by the partners, however, all such accounts shall bear the partnership name. All partnership funds shall only be deposited in accounts bearing the partnership name.

## *Designate Number of Partners to Sign Checks*

*Clause 4*

PARTNERSHIP CHECKS AND ACCOUNT WITHDRAWALS. All checks drawn on partnership checking accounts must be signed by at least _____ partners. All withdrawals of funds from other partnership accounts must be on the signature of at least _____ partners.

## EXPENSE ACCOUNTS

Only use one of these clauses in your partnership agreement to describe how partner expense accounts will be handled.

### *No Expense Accounts*

**Clause 1**

NO PARTNER EXPENSE ACCOUNTS. No partner shall have an expense account. Unless reimbursement is authorized by a majority vote of the partners, each partner shall personally be responsible for payment of expenses related to his or her usual business activities.

### *Equal Expense Accounts*

**Clause 2**

EXPENSE ACCOUNTS. Each partner shall receive an expense account of up to $_____ per month for actual, necessary and reasonable expenses incurred in the regular course of partnership business. Each partner shall keep a record of his or her expenses, and shall submit such record monthly for payment.

### *Unequal Expense Accounts*

**Clause 3**

EXPENSE ACCOUNTS. The partners listed below shall receive a monthly expense account in the amount indicated for actual, necessary and reasonable expenses incurred in the regular course of partnership business. Each such partner shall keep a record of his or her expenses, and shall submit such record monthly for payment.

| Partner | Amount |
|---------|--------|
| _____ | _____ |
| _____ | _____ |
| _____ | _____ |
| _____ | _____ |

## INSURANCE

You may use one or more of these clauses in your partnership agreement to describe how insurance matters will be handled.

### *Business Insurance*

**Clause 1** | INSURANCE OF BUSINESS. The partnership shall maintain policies of insurance to cover liability and business assets. Business asset insurance shall be sufficient to replace such assets. Liability insurance shall be in an amount determined by a majority vote of partners.

### *Life Insurance on Partners*

**Clause 2** | LIFE INSURANCE ON PARTNERS. The partnership shall maintain a life insurance policy on each partner in the face value of $_____. Said policy shall be an asset of the partnership.

### *Disability Insurance on Partners*

**Clause 3** | DISABILITY INSURANCE ON PARTNERS. The partnership shall maintain a disability insurance policy on each partner in the face value of $_____. Said policy shall be an asset of the partnership.

## PARTNERSHIP MEETINGS

This is a good clause to include in your partnership agreement, because it forces the partners to set aside a regular time to discuss partnership business. Fill in a description of when and where the meetings will take place, such as *on the first Tuesday of each month, at 7:00 p.m., at the partnership's place of business.*

PARTNERSHIP MEETINGS. In order to discuss partnership business, the partners shall meet _____ _____, or at such other times as determined by a majority vote of the partners.

## TRANSFER OF PARTNER'S INTEREST

Follow these rules when using the clauses.

- Choose only one clause between Clauses 3 and 4.
- Choose only one clause between Clauses 5, 6, and 7.
- Otherwise you may use both Clauses 1 and 2 with the others you choose.

### *Option of Partnership to Purchase*

**Clause 1**

OPTION OF PARTNERSHIP TO PURCHASE / RIGHT OF FIRST REFUSAL. In the event any partner leaves the partnership, for whatever reason including voluntary withdrawal or retirement, expulsion, incapacity, or death, the remaining partner(s) shall have the option to purchase said partner's interest from said partner or his or her estate. In the event any partner receives, and is willing to accept, an offer from a person who is not a partner to purchase all of his or her interest in the partnership, he or she shall notify the other partners of the identity of the proposed buyer, the amount and terms of the offer, and of his or her willingness to accept the offer. The other partner(s) shall then have the option, within 30 days after notice is given, to purchase that partner's interest in the partnership on the same terms as those of the offer of the person who is not a partner.

### *Option to Sell or Dissolve Partnership*

**Clause 2**

OPTION OF PARTNERSHIP TO SELL OR DISSOLVE PARTNERSHIP. In the event a partner leaves or receives an offer to purchase his or her interest as provided for in this agreement, and the remaining partner(s) do not exercise the option to purchase, the remaining partners have the option to put the entire business up for sale, or to dissolve the partnership.

### Valuation of Partnership (Basic)

*Clause 3*

VALUATION OF PARTNERSHIP. In the event the remaining partners exercise their right to purchase another partner's interest as provided above, the value of the partnership shall be the net worth of the partnership as of the date of such purchase. Net worth shall be determined by the market value of the following assets: all of the partnership's real and personal property, liquid assets, accounts receivable, earned but unbilled fees, and money earned for work in progress, and any goodwill of the business; less the total amount of all debts owed by the partnership.

**NOTE:** *Clause 3 includes the goodwill of the business in determining the valuation. This is a value assigned in many businesses to account for the value of the business' good name and reputation. If you do not wish to include goodwill when determining the value of the partnership, simply delete the phrase "and any goodwill of the business" from this paragraph.*

### Valuation of Partnership (By Appraisal)

*Clause 4*

VALUATION OF PARTNERSHIP. In the event the remaining partners exercise their right to purchase another partner's interest as provided above, the value of the partnership shall be determined by an independent appraisal. The cost of the appraisal shall be shared equally by the departing partner and the partnership.

### Payment in Cash

*Clause 5*

PAYMENT UPON BUY-OUT. In the event the remaining partners exercise their right to purchase another partner's interest as provided above, they shall pay the departing partner in cash for his or her interest within _____ days of the date of purchase.

### *Payment in Installments*

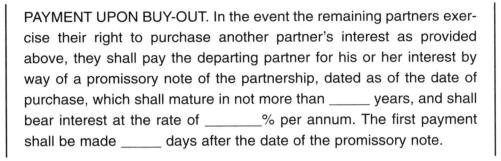

**Clause 6** | PAYMENT UPON BUY-OUT. In the event the remaining partners exercise their right to purchase another partner's interest as provided above, they shall pay the departing partner for his or her interest by way of a promissory note of the partnership, dated as of the date of purchase, which shall mature in not more than _____ years, and shall bear interest at the rate of _____% per annum. The first payment shall be made _____ days after the date of the promissory note.

### *Payment in Cash and Installments*

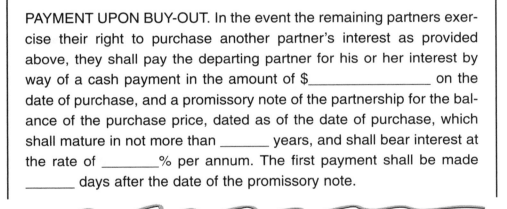

**Clause 7** | PAYMENT UPON BUY-OUT. In the event the remaining partners exercise their right to purchase another partner's interest as provided above, they shall pay the departing partner for his or her interest by way of a cash payment in the amount of $_____ on the date of purchase, and a promissory note of the partnership for the balance of the purchase price, dated as of the date of purchase, which shall mature in not more than _____ years, and shall bear interest at the rate of _____% per annum. The first payment shall be made _____ days after the date of the promissory note.

## EXPULSION OF A PARTNER

Sometimes it becomes necessary to get rid of a partner. This may be due to that partner's inability to get along with the other partners, or to his or her financial situation, or for many other reasons.

Only use one of these clauses in your partnership agreement.

Although these clauses provide that there may be no court challenge, there is always the possibility that a judge will declare that part of the agreement unenforceable.

### *Expulsion Upon Vote*

*Clause 1*

EXPULSION OF A PARTNER. A partner may be expelled by the unanimous vote of the remaining partners. Upon such expulsion, the expelled partner shall cease to be a partner and shall have no interest in the partnership or partnership property, except as otherwise provided in this agreement. Said partner's rights, powers and authorities, including the right to share in partnership profits, shall also cease. The expelled partner shall be considered a seller of his or her interest in the partnership as set forth in this agreement. In the event of any such expulsion, the partnership shall not be dissolved, but shall continue its business without interruption. The expulsion of any partner as provided above shall not be subject to mediation, arbitration, or review by any court.

**NOTE:** *This clause simply gives the other partners the authority to expel a partner, does not provide for automatic expulsion, and leaves much to the whims and personalities of the other partners.*

## *Automatic Expulsion for Specific Acts*

*Clause 2*

EXPULSION OF A PARTNER. A partner shall be expelled from the partnership for any of the following reasons:

1.   upon a unanimous vote of the other partners to expel a partner;

2.   when the partner files a petition for relief under the Bankruptcy Code;

3.   when the partner files for, or becomes subject to an order or decree of, insolvency under any state law;

4.   when the partner files for, consents to, or becomes subject to, the appointment of a receiver or trustee over any of his or her assets that is not vacated within _____ days;

5.   when the partner consents to, or becomes subject to, an attachment or execution of his or her assets that is not released within _____ days; or,

6.   when the partner makes an assignment for the benefit of creditors.

Upon the occurrence of any of the above events, the expelled partner shall cease to be a partner and shall have no interest in the partnership or partnership property. Said partner's rights, powers and authorities, including the right to share in partnership profits, shall also cease. The expelled partner shall be considered a seller of his or her interest in the partnership as set forth in this agreement. In the event of any such expulsion, the partnership shall not be dissolved, but shall continue its business without interruption. The expulsion of any partner as provided above shall not be subject to mediation, arbitration, or review by any court.

**NOTE:** *This clause gives circumstances under which expulsion is automatic, and makes it clear what conduct and situations will not be permitted for less chance of a court challenge.*

## OWNERSHIP OF BUSINESS NAME

The following clauses relate to who owns the name of the partnership. This can make a difference in the event the business is sold, or some partners want to continue in business with the advantage of the goodwill the name enjoys. Choose either Clause 1 or Clause 2. Clause 3 may be used along with Clause 1, if desired. However, do not use Clause 3 along with Clause 2.

### *Name Owned by Partnership*

**Clause 1**

PARTNERSHIP BUSINESS NAME. The business name of the partnership, _____, is owned by the partnership. No partner may use said name after leaving the partnership.

### *Name Owned by Other Than Partnership*

**Clause 2**

PARTNERSHIP BUSINESS NAME. The business name of the partnership,_____, is owned solely by _____, and not by the partnership.

PARTNERSHIP BUSINESS NAME. The business name of the partnership,_____, is owned solely by _____, and not by the partnership.

### *Name Owned by Majority of Partners Upon Dissolution*

**Clause 3**

PARTNERSHIP BUSINESS NAME. In the event the partnership is dissolved, the business name of the partnership,_____, is owned by a majority of the partners. No other former partner may use said name.

## ASSET OWNERSHIP

It is sometimes necessary or desirable to clearly state who owns certain assets. This is especially true in the case of intellectual property, trade secrets, patents, and copyrights. You may use some, but not all, of these clauses in your partnership agreement. Choose either Clause 1 or 2. Choose either Clause 3 or 4. Otherwise these may be used together.

### *Intellectual Property—Owned by Individual Partner*

*Clause 1*

OWNERSHIP OF INTELLECTUAL PROPERTY. It is agreed and understood that any partner who creates or develops intellectual property shall retain sole ownership of his or her intellectual property, which shall not become a partnership asset, PROVIDED, that the partnership shall have the exclusive use of any such intellectual property as long as the owner remains a partner. It is further agreed that such intellectual property may not be sold, assigned, licensed, or in any way transferred to any third parties by the partnership, without the written consent of the owner of the intellectual property.

### *Intellectual Property—Owned by Partnership*

*Clause 2*

OWNERSHIP OF INTELLECTUAL PROPERTY. It is agreed and understood that any intellectual property created or developed by any partner or partners relating to partnership business shall become the property of the partnership.

### *Patents—Belong to Partnership*

*Clause 3*

OWNERSHIP OF PATENTS. Any ideas or items developed by any partner or partners relating to partnership business that are subject to an application for patent protection shall become the property of the partnership, and shall be patented in the partnership name.

### *Patents—Belong to Individual Partner*

**Clause 4**

OWNERSHIP OF PATENTS. Any ideas or items developed by any partner or partners relating to partnership business that are subject to an application for patent protection shall become the property of the partner or partners who develop it, and not the property of the partnership; PROVIDED, that the partnership shall have the exclusive use of any such patent as long as the developing partners remain partners.

### *Copyrights*

**Clause 5**

OWNERSHIP OF COPYRIGHTS. All copyrighted materials in the partnership name shall be, and remain, partnership property. All copyrighted materials in the name of an individual partner shall be, and remain, that partner's individual property, and not partnership property.

### *Trade Secrets*

**Clause 6**

OWNERSHIP OF TRADE SECRETS. All trade secrets used or developed by the partnership, including customer lists, supply sources, and computer programs, shall be owned and controlled by the partnership.

## OTHER BUSINESS ACTIVITY AND
## NONCOMPETITION CLAUSES

You may not want one of your partners to be dividing his time between the partnership business and another business. Or you may already have another business which you want to maintain. Also, if one of your partners leaves the partnership you would not want him or her setting up a business to compete with you. These situations can be avoided by an appropriate *other business activity* or a *noncompetition* clause. Generally, the courts will only permit you to limit someone's activities for a reasonable period of time, and to a reasonable geographical area. What is reasonable may depend upon the nature of your business, so you may need to vary these paragraphs accordingly.

Only use one of these clauses in your partnership agreement.

### *Outside Business Activity Not Permitted*

*Clause 1*

OUTSIDE BUSINESS ACTIVITIES. All partners shall devote their full time energies to the partnership business, and shall not be actively involved in any other business as an employee, officer, director, agent, partner, agent, or stockholder, or in any other capacity. This paragraph shall not prohibit a partner from being a passive investor in any business as long as he or she is not actively engaged in, or exercising control over, such other business.

### *Outside Business Activity Permitted*

*Clause 2*

OUTSIDE BUSINESS ACTIVITIES. Each partner may engage in other business activities, including those which compete with the partnership.

### *Outside Business Activity Limited*

*Clause 3*

OUTSIDE BUSINESS ACTIVITIES. Each partner may engage in other business activities, as long as such other business activities do not compete with, or interfere with, the business of the partnership; and do not conflict with the partner's obligations and time commitments to the partnership.

***Outside Business Activity Specified***

*Clause 4*

OUTSIDE BUSINESS ACTIVITIES. Except for those business activities listed below, no partner shall be actively involved in any other business as an employee, officer, director, agent, partner, agent, or stockholder, or in any other capacity. This paragraph shall not prohibit a partner from being a passive investor in any business as long as he or she is not actively engaged in, or exercising control over, such other business.

Partner                                    Permitted Business Activity

_____        _____

_____        _____

***Agreement Not to Compete***

*Clause 5*

AGREEMENT NOT TO COMPETE. It is agreed and understood that no partner, upon leaving the partnership, may engage in any business or activity that would compete with, or is similar to, the business of the partnership. This prohibition against competing with the partnership shall continue for a period of _____ years after leaving the partnership, and shall be limited to engaging in a similar business or activity within _____ miles of the partnership's place of business.

## MEDIATION AND ARBITRATION

The cost of a court battle can be disastrous, and that is true even if you win. Furthermore, the court system is generally as unpredictable as the weather. Sometimes the courts can be avoided by having disputes resolved through mediation or arbitration. This is generally cheaper, and the resolution more satisfying to both sides.

*Mediation* is where an independent person tries to help the two sides reach an agreement. The mediator has no power to make a decision, or require anyone to do anything.

*Arbitration* is more like an informal court. Both sides present their position to the arbitrator, who then makes a decision.

Use Clause 1 with either Clause 2 or Clause 3. Do not use *both* 2 and 3.

### *Mediation*

**Clause 1**

MEDIATION OF DISPUTES. In the event of any dispute arising under this agreement, all partners agree that a resolution shall first be sought through mediation. As mediation is voluntary, all partners agree to cooperate with the mediator in attempting to resolve the dispute. It is agreed that _____ shall serve as mediator, and that if such person is unable or unwilling to serve as mediator another mediator shall be chosen by mutual agreement of the partners to the dispute. Mediation shall be initiated by a written request for mediation, which shall be delivered to the other partners and the mediator. Mediation shall commence within _____ days after the request for mediation is delivered. Any agreement reached at through mediation shall be reduced to writing, shall be signed by all of the partners, and shall be binding upon all of the partners. Any costs of mediation shall be shared equally by all partners to the dispute.

## *Arbitration—With One Arbitrator*

*Clause 2*

ARBITRATION. In the event of any dispute arising under this agreement which could not be resolved through mediation, all partners agree that a resolution shall be sought through arbitration. It is agreed that _____ shall serve as arbitrator. Arbitration shall be initiated by a written request for arbitration, which shall state the nature of the dispute and the requesting partner's position, and shall be delivered to the other partners and the arbitrator. Arbitration shall proceed as follows.

(1)   Within 3 days, the other partners shall have the right to deliver a response, which shall state the responding party's position, to the requesting party and to the arbitrator.

(2)   Within 7 days after receiving the response (or of the date a response was due), the arbitrator shall hold a hearing, at which time either party may present oral or written evidence. No partner may be represented by an attorney or any other third party.

(3)   The arbitrator shall issue a written decision within 7 days of the hearing date, which shall be delivered to both parties.

(4)   Any costs of arbitration shall be shared equally by all partners to the dispute.

## Arbitration - With Three Arbitrators

**Clause 3**

ARBITRATION. In the event of any dispute arising under this agreement which could not be resolved through mediation, all partners agree that a resolution shall be sought through arbitration. Arbitration shall be initiated by a written request for arbitration, which shall state the nature of the dispute, the requesting partner's position, and shall name one person to serve as an arbitrator. Such request shall be delivered to the other partners. Arbitration shall proceed as follows.

(1)  Within 3 days after receiving the request for arbitration, the other partners shall have the right to deliver a response, which shall name a person to serve as the second arbitrator, and may state the responding party's position. This response shall be delivered to the other party to the dispute.

(2)  Within 3 days after receiving a copy of the request and the response, the two designated arbitrators shall select a third arbitrator.

(3)  Within 7 days after selection of the third arbitrator, the arbitrators shall hold a hearing, at which time either party may present oral or written evidence. No partner may be represented by an attorney or any other third party.

(4)  The arbitrator shall issue a written decision within 7 days of the hearing date, which shall be delivered to both parties.

(5)  Any costs of arbitration shall be shared equally by all partners to the dispute.

## STANDARD CLAUSES

All of these clauses should be included in your partnership agreement. They will avoid many basic legal disputes. These are usually the last clauses before the signatures.

*Clause 1*

CONTINUITY OF PARTNERSHIP. In the event of a partner's voluntary withdrawal, expulsion, death, or incapacity, the partnership shall not terminate or dissolve, but shall continue its business without any break in continuity.

**NOTE:** *Clause 1 allows the partnership business to continue in the event of the withdrawal, expulsion, death, or incapacity of a partner. Under traditional partnership law, any of these events would have resulted in the end of the entire partnership; although continuation is allowed under the Uniform Partnership acts.*

*Clause 2*

GOVERNING LAW. This agreement shall be governed by the laws of

_____.

**NOTE:** *The name of your state should be inserted in the blank. Clause 2 will prevent one of the partners from filing suit in another state, which might have different ramifications depending upon the law of the other state, and would also cost the partnership more money to defend.*

*Clause 3*

SEVERABILITY. If any part of this agreement is adjudged invalid, illegal, or unenforceable, the remaining parts shall not be affected and shall remain in full force and effect.

**NOTE:** *Clause 3 prevents the entire partnership agreement from being declared void and unenforceable in the event one part of it is do declared.*

**Clause 4**　　BINDING AGREEMENT / NO OTHER BENEFICIARY. This agreement shall be binding upon the parties, and upon their heirs, executors, personal representatives, administrators, and assigns. No person shall have a right or cause of action arising or resulting from this agreement except those who are parties to it and their successors in interest.

**NOTE:** *Clause 4 makes the agreement clearly binding on the named classes of persons, and prevents anyone outside of one of those classes from pursuing any lawsuits or claims against the partnership.*

**Clause 5**　　ENTIRE AGREEMENT. This instrument, including any attached exhibits, constitutes the entire agreement of the parties. No representations or promises have been made except those that are set out in this agreement. This agreement may not be modified except in writing signed by all the parties.

**NOTE:** *Clause 5 prevents any partner from claiming there were other, verbal agreements made between the partners.*

**Clause 6**　　PARAGRAPH HEADINGS. The headings of the paragraphs contained in this agreement are for convenience only, and are not to be considered a part of this agreement or used in determining its content or context.

**NOTE:** *In the event of a lawsuit between partners, Clause 6 prevents a partner from using a paragraph heading to twist the meaning of the paragraph itself. Basically, it provides that it is the content of the paragraph, not the heading, that is to be followed.*

## ADMISSION OF NEW PARTNERS

Sometimes it becomes desirable to have a new partner join the partnership.

Only use one of these clauses in your partnership agreement.

### *Admission Upon Unanimous Agreement*

*Clause 1*

ADMISSION OF NEW PARTNERS. A new partner may join the partnership only with the unanimous written agreement of all of the partners, which shall include a revised agreement as to the sharing in profits and losses, and the ownership interests, of the partners.

### *Admission Upon Majority Agreement*

*Clause 2*

ADMISSION OF NEW PARTNERS. A new partner may join the partnership only with the written agreement of a majority of the partners, which shall include a revised agreement as to the sharing in profits and losses, and the ownership interests, of the partners.

## MANAGING PARTNER

Sometimes a partnership will be formed on the agreement that one partner will serve as the active business manager, with the other partners being *silent partners*.

These clauses may be used together in a partnership agreement.

**Clause 1**

DESIGNATION AND AUTHORITY OF MANAGING PARTNER.

_____ shall be designated the managing partner. The managing partner shall have sole authority to conduct and make decisions regarding the routine, day-to-day operations of the business; including but not limited to the hiring of employees and independent contractors, and the borrowing of money up to the sum of $_____, the signing of partnership checks and withdrawal of funds from partnership bank accounts, and the maintenance of partnership business and financial records. The managing partner shall not make any major decision without a majority vote of all the partners, a major decision being defined as

_____

_____.

**Clause 2**

SALARY OF MANAGING PARTNER. The managing partner shall be paid a salary of $_____ per _____, which shall be a partnership expense in determining profits and losses.

# INDEX